UNIVERSITY

THE AUTISTIC GUIDE

DR HARRIET AXBEY

EVERYTHING YOU NEED

UCAS · DECIDING ON A DEGREE · STUDENT FINANCE · GROUP PROJECTS · FINDING YOUR PEOPLE · FOOD · INTERVIEWS AND EXAMS · PEER SUPPORT · SPORTS · FRESHERS · REASONABLE ADJUSTMENTS · YEAR ABROAD

TO SURVIVE AND THRIVE

ILLUSTRATED BY
JONATHAN RAISEBOROUGH

University: The Autistic Guide
Everything You Need to Survive and Thrive

Published by:

Pavilion Publishing and Media Ltd
Blue Sky Offices
25 Cecil Pashley Way
Shoreham by Sea
West Sussex
BN43 5FF

Tel: +44 (0)1273 434 943
Email: info@pavpub.com
Web: www.pavpub.com

Published 2024

ISBN: 978-1-803882-54-3

Pavilion Publishing and Media is a leading publisher of books, training materials and digital content in mental health, social care and allied fields. Pavilion and its imprints offer must-have knowledge and innovative learning solutions underpinned by sound research and professional values.

Author: Dr Harriet Axbey
Editor: Mike Benge
Illustrations and cover design: Jonathan Raiseborough
Page layout and typesetting: Emma Dawe, Pavilion Publishing and Media Ltd
Printing: Independent Publishers Group (IPG)

For Hazel

About the author

Harriet completed her undergraduate teacher training degree in Primary Education in 2018, before moving onto her master's degree in Research Methods, and then a PhD in Education looking at neurodiverse interactions between Autistic and non-Autistic people. Her research interests include inclusive research practices and education, sexual and reproductive health, and neurodiversity. In her spare time, Harriet enjoys kayaking, camping, baking, and watching the birds in the fields behind her garden. She has also written a children's book called *My Brother Tom Has Superpowers*, based on her own experiences of growing up Autistic in a neurotypical world.

Acknowledgments

Firstly, I would like to thank all the Autistic people who contributed to this project, and my wonderful illustrator Jonathan Raiseborough for bringing the book to life.

Thank you to all the people who made my own time at university successful: my parents for driving me to many open days and interviews, Stephenson College at Durham University, and Jane Dove who helped give me the idea to write this book.

And thank you David, for all your love and support in helping me reach the end of my third and final degree!

Contents

All of the resources are available online at
www.pavpub.com/university-the-autistic-guide-resources
from where they can be downloaded and printed.

Timeline

These timings will vary a bit depending on your situation; your school may also have their own timeline, so use these as a rough guide only. They may also differ in Scotland, as some students start university after S5.

Year 12 (Lower 6th/Year 13 in Northern Ireland/S5 in Scotland)

Autumn-Spring:	Decide upon a degree, make a list of universities that interest you (see p.18).
All year:	Visit universities on their open days (see p.19).
Summer:	Start working on your personal statement (see p.23), narrow down your list of universities.

Year 13 (Upper 6th/Year 14 in Northern Ireland/S6 in Scotland)

Autumn:	Choose the universities you want to apply for and start your application (see p.22). If applying for medicine or Oxford or Cambridge, apply before mid-October.
Before January:	For all other subjects/universities, apply now.
Spring:	Apply for student loans (see p.33) and Disabled Student Allowance (see p.36). Attend interviews if applicable (see p.26). Receive offers (see p.29). Make your firm and second choices.
May:	The universities will need to let you know if your application has been successful by now.
Summer:	Arrange accommodation at your top choice university (see p.40).
June/July:	Check your vaccination record, get any jabs that you need to have (see p.59).
August:	Email the student support/disability support services to ask about moving into university a few days early (see p.50). Receive your results (if A-Level).
September:	Start packing! (see p.50)

First year at university

September/October:	Start at university. Register with a GP near your university (see p.59).
November/December:	Start considering where you want to live in your second year (see p.131).

Glossary

Autistic burnout:

This is a condition resulting from chronic stress and over-exertion without adequate support. It manifests as long-term exhaustion, loss of functioning, and a smaller window of tolerance.

Bank account interest:

Money the bank pays you for having money in an account with them. The higher the percentage, the higher the amount of money they give you. The more money you have in your account, the more interest you get.

Bursary/grant:

Money you are given that you do not have to pay back. You might be given a bursary or grant because of your postcode or household income, or because you are very good at a sport or other activity.

Campus university:

All university facilities are contained in one area, with students living on one site.

Catered:

Your accommodation has no kitchen, and the university or accommodation provider will supply your meals. You will go into a café or cafeteria to eat breakfast, lunch and dinner. They will usually wash up for you too. Most catered halls will not provide meals during the university holidays.

City university:

University facilities are spread out across a city.

Clearing:

Where you can apply for courses that still have spaces on them if you do not get into either of your chosen universities, or you decide you do not want to go to them.

Collegiate university:

A university divided up into several colleges where students study, sleep, or both.

Collusion:
When students work together to complete an assessment that should have been completed independently.

Conditional offer:
You have been accepted onto your course at the university providing you meet some conditions, normally achieving certain specified A-Level results.

Contract cheating:
When someone else completes an assessment for you. It is often in exchange for some form of payment, but not always.

Degree classification:
The grading levels used to describe attainment at degree level. For undergraduates, this goes from a First-class degree to an ordinary degree.

Dependent student:
Anyone under the age of 25 who has support from their birth or adoptive parents.

Doctoral study:
Typically, three or four years of full-time study above master's level, after which you can call yourself a doctor. There are different types, a PhD (Doctor of Philosophy) is the most common, but there are also EdD (Doctor of Education), and MD (Doctor of Medicine). Other doctorates exist, and other countries will have different names for doctorates also, but these are the most common.

Drug testing:
This is offered in some parts of the country and at some festivals. It is where someone will take the drug you have been given (pill, power etc.) and test it to see if it really is what you were told it is. It is then up to you if you take it. This is a safer way to do drugs but does not eliminate risk.

DSA:
Disabled student allowance is a **grant** given to disabled students.

En-suite:
A room with a bathroom attached to it that is just for the people in the room to use.

Estranged student:
Anyone who does not have the support of their birth or adoptive parents.

Extension:
When you are given extra time to work on an assignment past a deadline. This can be due to ill-health, personal circumstances, or other reasons.

Firm choice:
This is your first-choice university and the one you will go to if you meet the conditions.

Formative assessment:
Used to monitor learning and progress. It does not count towards a student's final grade, but can help them to see where they are at, academically.

Freshers' fair:
A gathering of clubs, societies and student groups in one place. There are often stalls for each group and freebies on offer. Some companies may also be there, such as employers, or the local gym, for example.

General allowance:
Disabled student allowance funding for things such as printing and photocopying.

Graduate Entry Medicine:
For students with a relevant undergraduate degree, it is possible to go onto a graduate programme of study where you will qualify with a degree in medicine in a shorter time than an undergraduate degree in medicine would take.

Guarantor:
Someone who agrees to pay your rent if you don't. This is often a parent or relative. Guarantor schemes exist if you are an estranged student.

Halls:
This is where students live, often just in their first year of their undergraduate degrees. They are called this because you will typically live on a hallway with lots of rooms coming off of it.

Hazing:
An activity which is humiliating or dangerous, in which someone is expected to take part in in order to gain group membership.

House share:
Several rooms in a house where you share a kitchen and bathroom.

Imposter syndrome:
When someone doubts their own talents, abilities or accomplishments; they may feel like they are a fraud and that someone will expose them as such.

Identity-first language:
This is language that puts the identity of the person before the subject. Examples include: Autistic person, gay man, dyslexic woman. This is compared to person-first language, where the subject comes first, such as: a man with Autism or a person with dyslexia.

Independent student:
Anyone over the age of 25, or who is under 25 and **estranged**.

Insurance:
A guarantee from a company that they will give you compensation (in the form of money, a repair, or a new object) in the case of loss, damage, illness, or death, in return for a one-off or regular payment.

Insurance choice:
This is your second-choice university, which you will go to if you don't meet the conditions of your firm choice.

Integrated master's:
Instead of doing an undergraduate degree followed by a master's degree, you can take one, longer degree which combines the two.

Junior common room (JCR):
Refers to both a physical space, often with its own bar, and the group of students that use it. Students are from the same college or accommodation halls, and JCRs are often run by elected students, organising events and social opportunities.

Lecture:
A class where an educator, a lecturer, talks to a large group of students about a topic.

Loan:
Money you are 'lent' by a bank or company. You will need to pay this money back, most often 'with interest', which means you pay back more than they gave you to begin with.

Master's degree:

Typically, this is a one-year degree which is at the level above an undergraduate degree.

Mate crime:

When a perpetrator pretends to befriend a victim in order to exploit them financially, physically or sexually.

Paired bathroom:

You will share a bathroom with one other person whose room is next to yours. If you are in self-catered accommodation, you will share with the others in your flat or on your hallway.

Personal statement:

Part of the university application written by the student. It is their chance to talk about why they want to study for a particular degree. It is currently limited to 4,000 characters (letters and spaces).

Personal tutor:

An academic you meet with regularly to discuss your progress and any issues you might be having. Sometimes called an academic adviser. Not all universities offer this.

PGCert and PGCE:

Postgraduate certificates (PGCerts) are courses with fewer credits than a master's degree. A Postgraduate Certificate in Education (PGCE) is a teacher training course where you can gain Qualified Teacher Status (QTS), allowing you to teach in UK schools.

Placement year:

Sometimes called a year in industry, or a 'sandwich year', this is where you take a year off from academic studying to work in a relevant professional setting to gain work experience. Sometimes these are paid roles, sometimes you are expected to live off just your student loan.

Plagiarism:

This involves including any idea or any language from someone else in your work without giving due credit by citing and referencing the source.

Masking:

To hide, or camouflage, who you are or parts of yourself in order to fit in with those around you.

Neurodiversity affirming:
Believing in a strengths-based approach to neurodevelopmental differences such as Autism. This means celebrating differences and supporting people without trying to fix or cure them.

Non-medical helper allowance:
Disabled student allowance funding for one-to-one support from someone who can help you such as a study skills tutor.

Open day:
A day when a university is open to potential students to look around.

Overdraft:
Money you can spend when you don't have money. For example, if your overdraft is £1,000, and you have £100 in your account, you could theoretically spend £1,100. That doesn't mean you *should*, however.

Part-catered:
Not all your meals will be provided. For example, you might get given five dinners a week but will need to cook for the rest of the time.

Reasonable adjustments:
Changes made by an organisation to ensure their services are accessible to disabled people.

Referee:
The person who writes your reference, which is a supporting statement saying how you are a good student and giving a bit more information about you as a learner.

Referencing:
Providing a piece of work with a citation or mention of the source where the information or argument originated.

Reject offer:
You can reject an offer from a university if you do not want to choose it as your firm or insurance.

Self-catered:
You will have a kitchen and will be responsible for making all your own meals.

Seminar:
A class with a small group of students where discussions and activities take place. Sometimes called a tutorial.

Shared bathroom:
You will share a bathroom with others, typically those in your flat or on your hallway. These bathrooms typically have more than one toilet and shower. If you are in self-catered accommodation you will share with the others in your flat or on your hallway.

Shared room/twin room:
Two people share a bedroom. There will be two beds, and they are sometimes separated by a wall that doesn't reach the ceiling. If you are in self-catered accommodation, you will share with the others in your flat or on your hallway.

Specialist equipment allowance:
Disabled student allowance funding for items such as laptops, software or ergonomic set-up.

Spiking:
Adding alcohol or a drug to someone's drink, food, or body without them realising.

Standing order:
A regular payment between two bank accounts. It will come out automatically, e.g., on the 15th of every month.

Students' union:
A student organisation dedicated to social activities, student representation, and support of the students at the university. It usually has its own building, and its purpose is to promote the interests of students. They have different names across the UK, and can also be known as student associations, or guilds.

Studio:
An apartment where the kitchen is in the same room as the bedroom. It will also have a bathroom in a separate room.

Summative assessment:
Used to evaluate student learning formally, with grades counting towards the student's degree or final grade for the year.

Term-time only contract:

You can live in the room during the university terms, but not during the holidays.

Travel allowance:

Disabled student allowance funding for additional travel costs you have due to your disability or learning difference.

UCAS:

The Universities and Colleges Admissions Service is an independent charity that deals with admissions into higher education in the UK.

Unconditional offer:

You have been accepted onto your course at the university and do not need any particular results to start on that course.

Unsuccessful application:

You have not got into that university. If you receive five unsuccessful applications, you can sometimes apply for one more.

Window of tolerance:

The ideal emotional zone between hyperarousal and hypoarousal. In this zone, you can manage life and your emotions effectively.

Year abroad:

You spend one year of your degree in another country, either working or attending the university there.

52-Week contract:

You have access to your room for a whole year from the start date of your contract. This is unusual for student halls, which usually run contracts from around September to June.

Introduction

What is this book about?

This book is about how to survive and thrive at university as an Autistic person. Starting university is likely the biggest transition you will have faced, especially if you are moving away from home for the first time. This book will guide you through the process of deciding which universities to apply to, and then applying to them. It will then look at the parts of going to university you need to consider, such as where you are going to live. Next it will outline the summer before you start, and the first week of term, followed by some advice for keeping yourself safe and well, physically, mentally and academically, and offer some advice for finding friends and like-minded people, including other Autistic people, at university. Finally, it will look at what comes next after university.

At the end of the book, there is advice for parents and carers, as well as educators in schools and universities and others helping Autistic people with the transition to university life. There are then some useful appendices with tick lists, resources and further reading.

I hope this book will be useful to you in this exciting journey. I have interspersed some of my own accounts alongside testimonials from other Autistic people about their experiences of university and advice they might have.

Who is this book for?

This book is for you. Yes, you. You must have picked it up for a reason, which means you will find it useful. Primarily, of course, this is written for Autistic people starting university in the UK. You will find that a lot of the information is aimed at those leaving sixth form/college to live away from home or care for the first time. However, information aimed at mature students and those living at home is also included. If any parts do not feel relevant to you, feel free to skip them; this book is meant to be picked up and put down, not read from cover to cover.

Contributors

Throughout this book, you will hear from other Autistic people talking about their experiences of being at university: things they struggled with, and those they found helpful. I am incredibly grateful to everyone who took the time to contribute to this book, and I hope that you find their advice and first-hand experiences as useful and interesting as I did.

Many thanks to:

Clare Davis
Emma Yao
Katie
Lauren Smith
Luce
Nadine Jones
Philippa
Becca Selby
Sarah Gardiner
Sophia Christophi
Sophie Taylor-Davies
Stacey
Tracy Smith

Language

This book uses **neurodiversity-affirming** language, with **identity-first** language used throughout (except where contributors have used otherwise). This is because research shows that most Autistic people prefer this type of language. Within the Autism community (Autistic people, professionals, parents etc.), there is a lot of debate surrounding language, and some people feel very strongly about what words people should or shouldn't use. You are allowed to use whatever words you like to describe yourself, and should never feel pressured into defining yourself based on what someone else says. That being said, it is important to respect the words other people use to describe themselves too, especially if this is different to the language you use.

Neurodiversity affirming: Believing in a strengths-based approach to neurodevelopmental differences such as autism. This means celebrating differences and supporting people without trying to fix or cure them.

Identity-first: Language that puts the identity of the person before the subject. Examples include: Autistic person, gay man, dyslexic woman. This is compared to **person-first** language where the subject comes first, such as: man with autism or person with dyslexia.

A final note

All information in this book is accurate at the time of writing. However, over the last few years we have seen leaders and governments come and go, and with each one we have experienced changes in the policies surrounding universities, and education more generally. When you read this, A-Levels may have been replaced with the next new qualification, student finance may look very different, One Direction may have reunited, and we will probably all have flip phones again. So, always check your information before acting on it.

Chapter 1: Deciding what and where to study

When you first sit down with the internet at your fingertips and thousands of possible courses, at over a 100 different universities, it can be exciting and overwhelming. This chapter will guide you through the deciding process, where you will narrow down these thousands of options into four of five final choices, before narrowing it down further to one or two. The chapter will go through what to expect at an open day, and then how to prepare for interviews and exams if you need to take these. It will briefly touch on the UCAS process, although the UCAS website itself has a wealth of information on this and is the best source of up-to-date information. If you have already applied and been accepted onto your course, you can skip most of this chapter.

Deciding on a degree

The deciding process often begins with choosing which degree course you would like to study. However, some people may have a very strong preference for a particular university, or type of university, and so their journey to deciding starts here. There is no right or wrong order to decide these things, however it is advisable to choose your course before you choose your university, as passion for your subject is greatly important if you are going to be studying it for at least three years. Many degrees will have subjects you need to have studied at A-Level, for example, for a physics degree you will most likely be asked for both physics and maths to a certain level. Some degree courses go further and ask for more subjects; this is to ensure that everyone starts with the level of knowledge required to begin the first-year course. Some degrees will not have required subjects but you may find certain A-Levels more useful than others. For example, for a degree with many written assignments, having an A-Level that focuses on essay writing, such as English or History, will help you in this area.

Most undergraduate degrees are three years long, however there are some exceptions. You can do a **placement year/year in industry, a year abroad**, or an **integrated master's**.

> **Placement year:** Sometimes called a year in industry, or a 'sandwich year', this is where you take a year off from academic studying to work in a relevant professional setting to gain work experience. Sometimes these are paid roles, sometimes you are expected to live off just your student loan.

> **Year abroad:** You spend one year of your degree in another country, either working or attending the university there.

> **Integrated master's:** Instead of doing an undergraduate degree followed by a master's degree, you can take one, longer, degree which combines the two. This is common in STEM subjects, and student finance usually treats it as an undergraduate degree, saving you money on doing a master's at an extra cost.

These are all really good options if you can take them, as they will give you more experience and make you more employable after you finish university. You can often switch out of a four-year degree onto a three-year course, so if you think you might want to do a longer degree, my advice would be to apply, as it is much harder to switch onto a different degree.

Foundation degrees

Foundation degrees are typically one year in length and provide an introduction to degree-level studies, primarily for those who did not receive the required grades to start in Year 1 of their chosen course. They are also useful for those with non-standard qualifications, or those who have missed time from school due to ill-health or other reasons. However, there are other reasons for deciding upon a foundation year, as explained by Clare:

'I decided to do a foundation year even though I had achieved the A-Level grades to skip this extra year. After a turbulent secondary education with several gaps and failures, and knowing that transitions are challenging for me, I felt that I would benefit from an extra year at university to adjust to this new environment academically, socially and emotionally. On paper, my foundation year was a disaster – I underachieved academically, often missed classes, struggled to regulate my emotions and didn't make any close friends. Working through these challenges in a foundation year was ultimately very helpful, as it made me better equipped for the 'important' years of my degree. Due to the lower academic pressure in foundation year, I had space to learn on my own terms and develop a real passion for my subject, which has sustained me through the tougher parts of my degree. This year also included more explicit teaching of academic skills, which I found particularly helpful as an Autistic person with a patchy prior education and need for clarity. By the time I started first year, I was more confident, academically and socially, and had a better understanding of my needs at university.'

Clare Davis, *Autistic psychology student*

As we can see from Clare's experiences, she chose to do a foundation year to help her transition to university. Now this will not tally with everyone's experience; many people find their foundation years useful but highly academically challenging after being out of education for many years, furthermore, not everyone may want to pursue this option, or want to spend the extra money required for an additional year at university, but foundation years can be useful for many. What is inspiring about Clare is she chose the best option *for her*, and this should be at the heart of all of your decisions.

Which university do I apply to?

Once you know what you want to study, you then need to choose a university. With over 150 in the UK to choose from, this can seem a little daunting. There are different types of universities to choose from, with '**campus universities**' having all the facilities in one place, and '**city universities**' being spread out across a city. There are pros and cons to both types of university. A campus university can have more of a community feel and can be less overwhelming as everything you need is in one place. These universities might have shops, bars, and even banks on site, meaning you never need to leave! However, this can feel claustrophobic for some, and in terms of nightlife, they may leave those wanting to have varied nights out wishing there was more to do. The lack of choice for shops may also be a problem for some Autistic people who like to have certain brands regularly, and these campuses are sometimes far away from towns and cities.

A city university may offer more variety in terms of things to do, and you will come into contact with more people not at your university; some city universities share cities with other universities, so you can meet students studying at other institutions. It can also be helpful to not live, work and play all in one place, as sometimes the separation of these things helps Autistic people to organise their life into parts. However, city universities can be overwhelming, as you have the hustle and bustle of daily city life to contend with, public transport to navigate, and sometimes much further distances between buildings.

Some consider the age of a university worth thinking about, with newer institutions, or those that used to be polytechnics (these were colleges where people could get a degree or train for a vocational subject, which became universities in 1992). Most cities will have one university that was an older university, and one that was a polytechnic, e.g. Sheffield and Sheffield Hallam, Manchester and Manchester Metropolitan, or Newcastle and Northumbria. These former polytechnics are sometimes looked down on for not being as 'prestigious' as the older universities. It is a well-touted fact that Oxford University is older than the Aztec Empire, but whether older is always better must be up to you to decide. Many universities that were established in the 20th Century have climbed the league tables very fast, so if you do care about where a university ranks in the charts, don't base your judgement purely on how old it is or whether it was a polytechnic.

Another type of university is a **collegiate university**, which is divided up into colleges, where students might live, study or both. There are 13 collegiate universities in the UK, helpfully all with different meanings of the word collegiate, and with different numbers of colleges. Queen's University Belfast only has two colleges, whereas the University of Oxford has 39. Some collegiate universities' colleges mainly provide accommodation and student support, such as the University of York and Durham University, whereas others offer different courses in different colleges such as the University of Arts London. The University of London is made up of several colleges which are treated as individual universities in their own right, including King's College London and University College London (UCL). Each university's website should detail what they mean by a college and will help you to make decisions about which college you should apply to.

When it comes to choosing a university to study at, write down a list of things you consider essential for your degree, and a list of things that are 'desirable' (in an ideal situation you'd have them, but it's not the end of the world if they're not there). This will help you narrow down your search, things you could include are: course requirements, distance from family/friends, possibility of doing a placement/year abroad, campus facilities, type of campus, and type of halls. An example list is below, and a template for your own list can be found at the back of the book.

Example list for deciding on a university:

Essential:

■ Option to do a year abroad on my course.

■ Catered halls on campus.

■ Campus university – not spread out over a city.

■ Within two hours' drive of my parents/carers.

Desirable:

■ Gym within walking distance of my halls.

■ Option to be in quiet halls/alcohol-free halls.

■ Rowing team at university.

Once you have your list, look at universities within your remit, and make a second list of universities you want to visit on an open day. Once you've visited, make sure to write down what you think of the university in case they all start to blur into one and you forget your impression of it! Use the table at the back of this book to help you gather your thoughts.

'The first thing I thought about when I was picking a university was to look for somewhere that wasn't too big. At 17, I did not know I was Autistic, but I knew I was Visually Impaired and that I was Neurodivergent (Dyspraxia and Dyscalculia).

My first choice was Media at a small university, all on one campus. Allowing me to live on campus in my first year and nearby in the following years.

The university seemed really supportive of my needs. We attended an open day and as soon as we arrived it felt the right place. The atmosphere was warm and welcoming. They invited us for an additional campus →

visit with the Head of Disability Support. We were also introduced to the Media, Film and Culture Department which was really helpful.

The experience backed up what was written in the prospectus – you are a name, not a number.

The support from the lecturers was wonderful, nothing was ever too much. We had conversations about my Disability and how they could support me. The university allowed me to get a great university experience and gave me support throughout my time there.'

Philippa, *Autistic media studies student*

Distance from friends and family may be very important to you, especially if to visit them you may need to get several trains or even fly to a different part of the country. However, it is also important to find the right fit for you. When I first started looking at universities, I wanted to be a two-hour drive from my parents' house, but I ended up at a university six hours away! Don't restrict yourself to certain locations before you consider the university itself. Visiting the university for an open day is a great way to find out whether the distance is appropriate for you.

Open days

An open day is your chance to look around the university. There are several types of open day, and it is important to visit at least once before you decide on a final university. Not everyone can afford to do this of course, however many universities offer reimbursement of costs for visiting, which is something to consider, and some do online open days, although these will not give you as good an idea of what the in-person experience will be like of course.

> **Open day:** A day where a university is open to potential students to look round.

The first type of open days are pre-offer days: these are aimed at those in Year 12, or early in Year 13, and will try to convince you to go to that university. These will have general talks on university life, tours of the campus, information on accommodation etc. The post-offer open days will also have these, but as their purpose is to persuade you to put them as your first choice once you have an offer, these open days will often focus on your particular subject and offer taster sessions in your department.

'The one thing I learned over time was that the most important pre-application task was to visit every possible university that had the course choice I was interested in. By visiting before I applied, I was able to test many things, whether the commute would be possible, whether I liked the campus and what their support was like for Autistic students like me. Although more commonly students visit the universities after they apply, I felt doing this a year before gave me insight prior to the application process.'

Sarah Gardiner (she/her), *Autistic student*

You can choose to attend an open day on your own, with friends/peers, or with a parent/guardian. There are benefits to each of these: on your own, you have the peace and quiet to explore in your own way, with friends or peers you can give each other ideas of what to see, although you may have different priorities. Going with a parent or guardian may be useful as they might pick up on things such as student welfare and accommodation standards that are easy to miss when first overwhelmed by a large campus – that is if you can deal with them talking about how much it's all changed since *they* were at university!

There will be the option to sign up to many different talks, this can be overwhelming for some, but helps others who (like me) like a timetable for every day. Don't worry if you don't have an exact plan for the day – just look around, get a feel for the place, stop for a cuppa in the students' union, and soak in the atmosphere. Apart from several new tote bags, branded pens, and headed notebooks (play your cards right and you'll never need to buy stationary again: I went to my open days in 2014 and I'm still working my way through stacks of branded post-it notes!), you will also gain an idea of what it would be like to attend university at this particular campus.

Take your time however: it can be an overwhelming, busy, loud, sensory nightmare. If universities offer a virtual option or a quieter day for Autistic students to look around, I would recommend this. Through contacting universities in writing this book, I found out that many offer specific tours for Autistic students, and quiet rooms across campus. Send an email before you visit, or write in the 'access needs' box, or similar, that you are Autistic. Wear comfy shoes or walking boots, and take a water bottle – at school, I don't think I appreciated how close everything was to each other; on an open day, don't be surprised if you're walking over a mile between buildings you want to look at, and then back again for lunch.

Applying

You will likely begin your application in Year 12, especially if you are planning on applying for medicine, veterinary medicine or dentistry, or you are applying to Oxford or Cambridge universities. Even if you are not applying for any of these, I would recommend spending your summer holiday between Year 12 and Year 13 researching, so you come into the new school year with a clear idea of where you want to apply. If you are at school or college, you will apply through them. Applications to university are done through the UCAS (Universities and Colleges Admissions Service) system, rather than to individual universities. This means your application will be the same for all five universities you apply to.

> **UCAS:** The Universities and Colleges Admissions Service is an independent charity, and deals with admissions into higher education in the UK.

It is important to note that you can only apply to four universities if you are applying for medicine, dentistry, veterinary medicine or veterinary science. You can also usually only apply to one of the two out of the University of Oxford and the University of Cambridge.

Your application will be made up of many parts, including:

- Basic information (contact details, name, address etc.).
- Personal circumstances (e.g. have you been in care).
- Qualifications and education history.
- Employment history.
- Personal statement.
- Reference.
- Course choices.

The UCAS website has a wealth of information, so this section does not attempt to replicate that; rather, certain important sections have been chosen to focus on instead. The website also has tools where you can look at almost every course from across the UK, rank, and compare them, before narrowing it down to your five choices. I recommend having a play around with all the tools at your disposal, as they will help you to make informed choices and to build the best possible application.

'Applying for university can be a daunting experience. I had hesitations about applying as I was worried about the university's perceived perceptions they may have of Autism. With the support and positive encouragement from my employer, I put an application in.

For me, research was essential to complete prior to applying to a university, research is significant, making sure the university is the right one, especially for an Autistic person. First of all, researching all potential universities with the course available. I compared each university, their support systems and their stance on disability, specifically Autism.

Secondarily, I'd email the course leader to explain I had Autism. I asked for a meeting to find out if the course was suitable, and if they could accommodate my reasonable adjustments. This was really helpful as it allows you time to prepare any questions, the type of support that is needed for you to complete the degree. This reduced the anxiety of meeting the team in advance online. From this meeting we scheduled a day to attend campus. I had the team show me around campus, giving me the necessary information. This was great as it reduced my sensory experience and I was very impressed by the accommodations.

An important part of applying is the personal statement. This allows the university to gain an accurate picture of your background. Make sure you keep the personal statement to the correct length. The main pieces of information you should include are why you want to follow your chosen degree, what you want to do after completion of the degree, past experiences that have led you to want to undertake the degree, any relevant and current skills, and past and present experiences. Finally, any career goals or achievements you want to achieve in the future.'

Nadine Clara-May Jones, *Autistic student in Special Educational Needs and Additional Learning Needs (Autism)*

Personal statement

Arguably the most important part of your application is your personal statement, 4,000 characters to tell the universities who you are and why they should choose you. Start this early, as you will likely have many, many drafts before you submit. You don't need to start at the beginning – if you think of a sentence, write it down; you can sew them all together at a later date. Avoid clichés: quoting famous people or classic texts is commonly done, but the university would much rather hear your own words. Common phrases also include 'I have always had a passion for', 'ever since I was a child I have...', buy try to consider innovative ways of getting your point across.

> **Personal statement:** Part of the university application written by the student. It is their chance to talk about why they want to study for a particular degree. It is currently limited to 4,000 characters (letters and spaces).

You may not consider being Autistic a large part of who you are; after all, you are a complex, amazing human with many talents and traits. However, consider mentioning that you are Autistic in your statement as this will give universities a feel of who you are, and will also show that you may have overcome more challenges than your non-Autistic peers during your school years. You have no obligation to tell anyone that you are Autistic, however, and if you don't want to disclose this, you do not have to.

Whatever you choose to write, make sure you write it in your own voice. There are many templates out there, and you can even use Artificial Intelligence (AI) programmes to draft an outline for you (but not write it for you!), and these can be helpful as a skeleton for you to work with. However, make sure that the final statement sounds like you, rather than a robot version of 'the perfect student'. The admissions staff will be reading thousands of personal statements; the best way to make yours stand out is to be yourself.

Finally, the personal statement is one part of your application, and you have lots of information about yourself within the rest of it. Avoid repeating information, for example, they can see that you got a Level 8 in English literature at GCSE, so you do not need to state this in your personal statement as well. Save your characters, as you will come to realise that 4,000 is not very many at all!

Tips for a great personal statement:

- Avoid clichés and common quotes.
- Consider mentioning you are Autistic.
- Let your own voice come through.
- Don't repeat information you have provided elsewhere in your application.

References

Throughout your life, you will need to ask people for references, but your university application may well be the first time you do this. A staff member at your school or college will write a statement giving information about you. This can include things like attendance, behaviour, attitude to learning, and attainment in certain subjects. They can also include information about struggles you've overcome, and your resilience or achievements. You can normally choose who gives your reference, it does not have to be your form tutor; if you have a closer relationship with the SENCo or a member of support staff, you may want to consider asking them to write it. They may also be writing fewer references, so they can make it more personal to you.

You can be involved in writing of reference; if there are things you want them to mention, make a bullet-pointed list and give it to the referee as this will help them to gather their thoughts and to remember what to write.

> **Referee:** The person who writes your reference, which is a supporting statement saying how you are a good student, and giving a bit more information about you as a learner.

'No matter which time I applied I always worried whether my choice and my personal statement matched or that the admissions person would see more than just my grades.

An important aspect to the application is to make sure that you choose a referee who knows you well and who you trust to give an accurate picture of you. This does not have to be the guidance teacher but could be any teacher at your school. This helps the university have a more accurate picture of you.'

Sarah Gardiner, *Autistic student*

It is an open secret that people are sometimes asked to write their own references for job or university applications, which the referee then signs, although this is frowned upon. However, you can give pointers to your referee – after all, this is your future, and they will probably appreciate being reminded of some of your achievements and struggles over the years.

Interviews and exams

Some programmes will require you to attend an interview or an exam, or even both, after you have submitted your application. This may be in person or online, and you should be given lots of information in advance about the process. Universities such as the University of Oxford and the University of Cambridge set their own exams for some courses, and certain degrees will require you to take standardised tests. For example, most medicine and dentistry courses will require you to pass either the University Clinical Aptitude Test (UCAT) or the BioMedical Admissions Test (BMAT) in order to gain a place on that course.

Medicine, teacher training, and creative subjects such as art and music usually require an interview for admission. In the case of teacher training and medicine, a DBS will often be required to start the course, and you will need to bring the documents needed for this. There are sometimes additional tasks on the day in addition to the interview itself, such as a writing or presentation task with a group of other applicants. Contact the university in advance to make sure you have all the information needed to do your best on the day. Letting them know you are Autistic is your choice, but it may help you to get the adjustments you need to perform at your best ability.

When it comes to the day of the interview or exam, I found it best to arrive at least an hour early to make sure I was in the right place. Once I'd arrived, I could look around, and I usually sat in the café on campus, calming myself and re-reading the information about the subject, the course, and the content we would be studying. Be prepared for the day, with everything you might need and plenty to eat and drink. One university for which I attended an interview made a note of who was on time and whether they had all the documents and photocopies needed for their DBS to be completed, or if they had to have photocopies made by the admin team. I don't know how they used this information, but it would be prudent to be in their good books from the start!

Dressing smart but comfortable is ideal: you don't want to be fiddling with uncomfortable tags or buttons when you need to be concentrating on what you are saying or writing, and you want to give the impression you are serious about applying, so something like a suit or smart dress is good. At the end of the day, what you say is more important than what you wear, but dressing smart may also help you to get into the mindset of the day.

During an interview, it is good to bring up details of certain modules you are looking forward to taking, e.g. 'What I really love about this university is that I can take the ancient civilisation modules in Year 2. I think I would love to do my dissertation on teaching Ancient Greece to young children.' Showing you have a detailed knowledge of the course itself will make you stand out and show you have a passion for your subject. Approach every interview as if it is your first-choice university – even if it is in fact your least favourite of the five! If you want to go the extra mile, look at who will be interviewing you; if their field is experimental psychology, mention which part of that topic you are interested in, or read one of their papers. Some people believe it is bad to 'suck up' to your interviewers, however it is incredibly flattering to have someone read your work, and it shows initiative and genuine interest in the course to do the extra research into these areas.

Have an idea of what you want to do with your degree; it's okay if you don't know yet, but if you think maybe you might use your languages degree to be a foreign correspondent for a news company, say this in the interview. This shows you have thought ahead, but also that you value their degree as useful and important. Bring in your own experience to the interview, whether it be topics you did in your A-Levels, a specific essay you enjoyed writing, work experience you did, or a place you visited that inspired you. Make the interviewer/s see that you are the right person for the course because you already fit into the subject area.

Be knowledgeable about the subject you want to study; you may not have studied it before, so read around the topic and bring up some of the main theorists and big names in the field. For example, 'I would love to learn more about Montessori and her methods, as the school I did my work experience in had a Montessori nursery, and I think the approach really helped with the children's development'. Knowing how to pronounce key terms and names of theorists is also important, I remember during my interview preparation it was pointed out I had been pronouncing Piaget wrong for two years!

Top tips for interviews:

■ Dress the part: smart is best.

■ Arrive early and prepared.

■ Bring up details specific to your course.

■ Plan ahead, say what you will do with this degree.

■ Bring in your own experience.

■ Swot up on your subject.

For exams, the guidance will be much the same as for your A-Levels. Firstly, remember supplies like pens and pencils (and a regulation calculator if needed), a bottle of water, and a snack. Bring any information you need like your UCAS number or your invitation to the day, as a hard copy if you can, in case your phone dies. Much like with the interview advice, contact them in advance to discuss accommodations such as doing the exam in a separate room, having rest breaks, or extra time. At the end of the day, they are testing your ability in a subject, not your ability to be uncomfortable for an hour, so asking for these things is a good idea.

Getting your offers

After your application, or after your exam/interview if you attended these, you will start to hear back from the universities you applied to. Some universities take longer than others, sometimes they take a week, sometimes they take months, it really is a waiting game, and you might find yourself checking UCAS daily to see if there have been updates. Universities have to let you know by mid-May. There are three types of responses you can receive from your application:

Conditional offer: You have been accepted onto your course at the university, providing you meet some conditions, normally achieving certain A-Level results.

Unconditional offer: You have been accepted onto your course at the university and do not need any particular results to start on that course.

> **Unsuccessful application:** You have not got into that university. If you receive five unsuccessful applications, you can sometimes apply for one more.

Do not make any decisions until you have all your offers come through, as there are some things to consider. An unconditional offer may look appealing, as it takes the stress off your exams at the end of the year, however, make sure it is the university you definitely want to attend and that you are not just choosing it for this reason. Additionally, having an unconditional offer does not mean you should not do your best in your exams, as employers may look at your results in the future.

Sometimes you may be given what is called a 'contextual offer'. This is an offer that is lower than what they normally ask for because they are taking into account your circumstances, e.g. a negative experience you have had, or an extra course you have gone on.

There are three decisions you can make with your offers:

Firm choice: This is your first-choice university and the one you will go to if you meet the conditions (if they set any). This is where you will apply for accommodation and finance.

Insurance choice: This is your second-choice university, which you will go to if you don't meet the conditions of your firm choice.

If you do not meet the conditions of either your firm or insurance choices, you can go through clearing after you have your results.

Reject offer: You can reject an offer from a university if you do not want to choose it as your firm or insurance. Be 100% sure before you reject any offers.

Always make sure your firm choice offer is asking for higher results than your insurance offer, otherwise, if you do not meet the requirements, you won't get into either. Some people like to have an insurance offer with much lower entry requirements, to ensure they have a solid back-up if they don't get the results for their firm offer. It is important to note that, if you accept an unconditional offer, you do not get an insurance offer. Some universities will give you a conditional offer, which changes to unconditional if you put them as your firm choice.

Clearing: Where you can apply for courses that still have spaces on them, if you do not get into either of your chosen universities, or decide you do not want to go to them.

'If you have received a conditional acceptance, I would still email the administrator to begin your own preparation and find ways to distract yourself until your exam results are through. When your exam results come through, remember that these are not the end of the world. If you have just missed your conditions, don't panic! Contact your chosen university and speak to them. In a lot of cases, you will still have your place, this is due to some places being held for students who chose the institution as a second choice and then do not take up their place. Universities want full courses, so if you miss your condition the first thing to do is call them.'

Sarah Gardiner, *Autistic student*

Deciding all this can seem daunting, so take some time to think about all your options. You might even decide you don't want to go to any of the universities you have offers from, and that you want to wait and go through clearing. Talk to people around you and look back at the notes you made about each university from your open-day visits.

Chapter 2: Getting ready

Student finance

Financing your degree is the next thing to consider after you have applied for university. There are different types of loans available in the UK, maintenance and tuition, and these come from student finance. There are different funding sources depending on where in the UK you live: for England this is Student Finance England (SFE), for Scotland it is the Student Awards Agency Scotland (SAAS), for Northern Ireland it is Student Finance NI, and for Wales, it is Student Finance Wales/Cyllid Myfyrwyr Cymru.

> **Loan:** Money you are 'lent' by a bank or company. You will need to pay this money back, most often 'with interest', which means you pay back more than they gave you to begin with.

> **Bursary/grant:** Money you are given that you do not have to pay back. You might be given a bursary or grant because of your postcode or household income, or because you are very good at a sport or other activity.

A maintenance loan is for your living costs; this gets put directly into your bank account and you can spend it on rent, food, books and everything you need to get by at university. A tuition fee loan is just for the cost of your course and will go directly to the university, not into your bank account. The types of loan available depend on where you live, for example if you are Scottish and applying for a Scottish university, you will not need a tuition fee loan as tuition is free for Scottish students. Northern Ireland, Scotland and Wales offer grants and/or bursaries in addition to loans; this is money you do not have to pay back. Student Finance England does not offer grants anymore; however, you may be able to get them from other funding sources. The amount of money you get may depend on many different factors such as:

- Your age.
- Your parents/carers income.
- Your postcode.
- Whether you have children.
- If you have certain disabilities.
- Your course.
- If you will be living at home during your degree.
- Whether you will be living in London.
- If you are married.
- Whether you are estranged from your parents.

If you already have a degree or equivalent, it is unlikely you will get funding for tuition or maintenance.

The process of applying for student finance can take up to eight weeks, so make sure you apply early so you don't miss the deadline (usually in the May before you start). This is especially important if your application might encounter hurdles, for example if you are a care leaver, estranged student or mature student. There is often added paperwork and bureaucracy for these students, for example if you have been involved with social services, but are now over 18, you may need to contact adult social services, to contact child social services, so that they can provide evidence of this for student finance. Unfortunately, the system is not always easy for those who most need it to be. You can call the student finance numbers for advice, but be aware that the closer to the deadline you get, the longer the wait times. Additionally, they will not talk to parents or carers without your express permission, so be aware of this if you need support making phone calls.

As mentioned, a loan with interest means you will end up paying back a lot more than you originally borrowed. However, don't let this put you off getting student finance for your time at university as it is not like a normal loan. For example, I currently owe £50,000 from my three years as an undergraduate, which looks like an awful lot of money! However, I am very unlikely to ever repay all of this, as it is wiped after 30 years. I currently pay back £14 a month, which comes straight out of my paycheck, and I didn't have to start paying any of it until I had a job earning over £27,000. Be aware that this is my own example from Student Finance England and starting university in 2015, but it gives you an idea of how it works.

Once you have an offer from a university, you may be able to apply for bursaries at your chosen university. These could be based on your circumstances, such as coming from a low-income household, leaving care, or living near the university. There are also bursaries for students with certain skills, like sporting ability, or being able to play the organ (they will probably ask you to play it at events!). Have a look on the university website and apply for as many as you can.

Estranged students

If you are under 25 when you apply for your course, you will be considered a **dependent student** and the income of your parents or adoptive parents will be taken into account when deciding how much money you will be given. However, if you are under 25 and **estranged**, you can apply as an **independent student**.

Estranged student: Anyone who does not have the support of their birth or adoptive parents.

Dependent student: Anyone under the age of 25 who has support from their birth or adoptive parents.

Independent student: Anyone over the age of 25, or who is under 25 and estranged.

Unfortunately, there are certain conditions you must meet to meet their definition of estranged. For example, if you do not have a social worker and you have not been in care in the last few years, you will often need to not have had any contact with your birth or adoptive parents for at least 12 months before your application. However, there are other instances in which you can be considered an independent student if you are under 25: if you are orphaned, married, divorced, or widowed, have children, or can show you have been financially independent for at least three years. A 'Confirmation of Estrangement' form will need to be completed, and this can be done by a social worker, police officer, teacher, doctor, or other member of the community who knows about your situation and is deemed trustworthy to report on it. The charity Stand Alone has excellent resources for estranged students, and the UCAS website can help you find out if you will meet the requirements for estranged/independent student status. Many Autistic people are estranged for a variety of reasons and attend university without any trouble. Reach out to charities and organisations that can help you get as much support as possible to help you thrive.

Applying for DSA

Disabled student allowance is a **grant** given to disabled students and those who require additional support with their studies. You can apply for DSA if you are impacted by a disability, learning difference, chronic illness or mental health condition. You will need to show evidence of any of these in order to access the funding. Having your Autism diagnosis will usually be all the evidence you need. If you are in the process of getting a diagnosis, talk to your doctor about getting a letter explaining that this is your situation.

Apply as soon as possible for DSA. You can do this when you apply for student finance. If you are not applying for student finance, you can apply for DSA separately. To receive DSA, you will have a needs assessment, online or in person, to determine what support you need. The application process is slightly different depending on which part of the UK you live in, so check you are applying in the right system. See the resources section for links to the different DSA providers across the UK.

'I applied for Disabled Students Allowance (DSA) as part of my student finance application. The process was fairly straightforward – I had to provide evidence of meeting the criteria and then arrange a needs assessment with one of their advisers. The appointment went through everything DSA could provide, and we discussed what would be helpful. The main outcomes were being allocated a mentor at my university disability service and a part-funded laptop with supportive software. This included software for speech-to-text, lecture recording and note taking, and referencing, and I was given training in how to use all of it. I was also provided with a printer, with reimbursement for paper and ink, and was offered a travel allowance for taxis to university if public transport was inaccessible. My initial application was on the basis of anxiety and depression, but if I'd had my Autism diagnosis at that point, I would have been able to access additional support and some other software. All of this remained in place throughout my time at university, so I never had to reapply. The company who supplied the laptop and software, and provided the training, were also very helpful and responsive with any issues I had.'

Katie, *Autistic chemistry student*

There are four types of support you can get from DSA, these are:

Specialist equipment allowance: funding for items such as laptops, software or ergonomic set-up.

Non-medical helper allowance: funding for one-to-one support from someone who can help you such as a study skills tutor.

General allowance: funding for things such as printing and photocopying.

> **Travel allowance:** funding for additional travel costs you have due to your disability or learning difference.

You may not feel like you need to apply for DSA, or you may feel that you won't meet the requirements for the support. There is no requirement to apply, and many Autistic students do not take up DSA. However, having as much support as possible can help you to achieve what you want to and make your life easier while at university, so it is worth considering what you might need. As Katie explained, you can receive a variety of the four types of funding, depending on your needs, and your needs assessment can help you determine what will be best for you. Take all the support you can get, even if you end up not needing all of it for the full duration of your course, too much is better than not enough, and you will not be taking it away from anyone else by asking for support.

Insurance

Welcome to the endlessly boring world of insurance. Over the course of your lifetime, you will be plagued by insurance costs as, it turns out, you can insure anything from your TV, to your car, to your own body. Allegedly 37,000 people in the UK have even taken out insurance against alien abduction! While at university, there are very few insurance costs you need to worry about, as most things will be covered already by the university or accommodation provider. However, it is worth considering insuring certain items such as your phone, laptop, or bike, in case they are lost or damaged. Some accommodations do not include contents insurance, which is insurance for everything that is inside the property (furniture, your belongings etc.), so you may need to pay for this yourself. For objects, it is worth checking if you are covered under your parent's/carer's insurance; if you will be returning to their property over holidays, sometimes your items are protected while you are away at university. Check the small print as you may save some money here.

> **Insurance:** A guarantee from a company that they will give you compensation (in the form of money, a repair, or a new object) in the case of loss, damage, illness, or death, in return for a one-off or regular payment.

Getting a student bank account

Once you have your results and a confirmed place at a university, you can open a student bank account. These are special accounts that are just for students, with the main difference between them and a usual current account being the generous **overdraft** you are given.

> **Overdraft:** Money you can spend when you don't have money. For example, if your overdraft is £1,000, and you have £100 in your account, you could theoretically spend £1,100. That doesn't mean you *should*, however.

Usually, if you do not have an overdraft, you cannot spend over the amount you have in your account, or you are charged a fee if you do. With an overdraft, this is not the case, and it can be tempting to go for the account with the biggest overdraft. However, you will still need to pay that money back at some point, usually after the course has finished, so my advice is to weigh up options, so you go with the one with the best overdraft, **interest rate**, and any other perks they offer you. Most will offer at least £1,000 overdraft anyway, but some offer up to £3,000. As you will be getting a large lump sum into your account with each maintenance payment, which will need to last you a while, you could be earning interest on this money while it is there. Other perks that banks might offer include cash, vouchers or a student railcard – a very useful thing to have if you will be getting the train at least twice a year for a longish journey to and from university, or regularly for short journeys. You can usually only open one student bank account, so make sure you choose which one carefully. To open a student bank account, you will need your offer letter from UCAS and your ID documents (e.g. passport).

> **Bank account interest:** Money the bank pays you for having money in an account with them. The higher the percentage, the higher the amount of money they give you. The more money you have in your account, the more interest you get.

Once you have finished your degree, be sure to upgrade to a graduate bank account, as these offer good interest rates and overdrafts. This does not always have to be with the bank you had your student bank account with, so shop around again for the best deals.

Accommodation

After you have submitted your UCAS application and received your offers, it is time to think about where you want to live while you are at university (although it is good to consider this before you apply too!) Many universities will begin sending emails out about their accommodation around May or June before you start, so keep an eye on your emails.

As you will have seen at the open days, there are many different types of accommodation available to you at university. I have detailed a couple below, but each university will have their own words for different types of accommodation, so check you understand what they mean by each term.

> **Halls:** This is where students live, often just in their first year of their undergraduate degrees. They are called this because you will typically live on a hallway with lots of rooms coming off of it.

Studio: An apartment where the kitchen is in the same room as the bedroom. It will also have a bathroom in a separate room.

En-suite: A room with a bathroom attached to it that is just for the people in the room to use.

Paired bathroom: You will share a bathroom with one other person whose room is next to yours. If you are in self-catered accommodation you will share with the others in your flat or on your hallway.

Shared bathroom: You will share a bathroom with others, typically those in your flat or on your hallway. These bathrooms typically have more than one toilet and shower. If you are in self-catered accommodation, you will share with the others in your flat or on your hallway.

Shared room/Twin room: Two people share a bedroom. There will be two beds, and they are sometimes separated by a wall that doesn't reach the ceiling. If you are in self-catered accommodation, you will share with the others in your flat or on your hallway.

House share: Several rooms in a house in which you share a kitchen and bathroom.

Catered: Your accommodation has no kitchen, and the university or accommodation provider will supply your meals. You will go into a café or cafeteria to eat breakfast, lunch and dinner. They will usually wash up for you too. Most catered halls will not provide meals during the university holidays.

Self-catered: You will have a kitchen and will be responsible for making your own meals.

Part-catered: Not all your meals will be provided. For example, you might get given five dinners a week and will need to cook for the rest of the time.

52-week contract: You have access to your room for a whole year from the start date of your contract. This is unusual for student halls, which usually run contracts from around September to June.

Term-time only contract: You can live in the room during the university terms, but not during the holidays.

Check your contract carefully, as some university accommodation will require you to completely move out of the room during the Christmas and Easter holidays. If you are estranged or do not want to go back to your parents or carers for the holidays, make sure you have somewhere to go during this time, or speak to your university and explain the situation.

Rental contracts

A rental contract is an agreement of terms between you and the place you are living. This will include the price of rent, and whether that price includes bills such as electricity, water, or a TV licence, or if you need to pay these separately yourself. It will also include additional conditions, such as that you agree to keep the place in a good condition, you will not smoke, and sometimes things like mowing the lawn. It also includes an agreement from the person or company you are renting from, such as that they will test the smoke alarms, be available if repairs need doing, and keep everything in working order. Reading your rental contract in full is essential, if boring, as if you do not keep up your terms of the contract you can be made to leave.

A few university halls, and most private accommodations like houses and flat shares, will require you to have a **guarantor**. Make sure you have an idea who you are going to put down and that they agree to this before you give their details. You will often need to provide a **deposit** for private renting, so be sure to have this additional money ready to pay.

Guarantor: Someone who agrees to pay your rent if you don't. This is often a parent or relative. Guarantor schemes exist if you are an estranged student.

To ensure you get your deposit back at the end of your tenancy, take photos at the very beginning and end of your tenancy so you can prove what damage was done before you moved in. Your students' union may offer a contract-checking service, or you can ask a parent or guardian to look at it for you, as once you sign it, it is very hard to get out of this agreement. As a tenant, you have certain rights, so it is worth knowing what these are, check out the resources section for links to services that can help you. Be wary of taking up a contract as a lodger, as you will have significantly fewer legal protections and they can ask you to leave at any time.

> **Deposit:** A lump sum taken by a landlord to be used to pay for any damages or non-payment of rent. You get this back at the end of the tenancy if it is not used for these purposes.

When it comes to who to live with, if you are living in university halls, you rarely get a say in this, although you are sometimes asked to put down preferences, such as whether you would like to live in a quiet flat, an alcohol-free flat, or one with only other women. Not all universities have these options, however, so it will vary from place to place.

In subsequent years, however, you will have more say in who you live with. If you are renting a house, you may get together with a group of other people to rent a house together with the required number of bedrooms. Be sure you are happy living with all of these people, and check the contract carefully: in some contracts, you rent just your room, but in others you all collectively rent a whole house, this means that if one person leaves without paying, the rest of the house are responsible for paying that person's rent.

Some universities allow you to live in their halls for the duration of your degree, especially if you have additional needs or medical requirements, and many Autistic people prefer this as it means you are closer to the university facilities and often have more support than if you are in a house share. Additionally, it can mean you stay in catered accommodation, which some people prefer if they do not like, or feel able to, cook for themselves all the time.

Often people are pressured into signing up for the next year's accommodation early in the first year of university. This can lead to many problems such as friends falling out and then not having anywhere to live, or someone deciding to have a year abroad, or dropping out, leaving the rest of their friends to frantically try and find someone to replace them. If you are unsure, wait, take the time to do your research, and be sure who you want to live with, as it can be very intense sharing a living space with others, especially as an Autistic person. Make sure you look around the house or flat, if possible, before you sign the contract, to ensure you will be happy living there.

Think about your sensory needs, for example, if the flat is above a shop that will have deliveries early every morning, will that be too loud for you? Have you decided which room you will each have, and if you are having a smaller room, are you having to pay the same as everybody else or will you pay slightly less? These are questions to ask yourself and those you wish to live with. You may want to live with people because you want to remain friends with them, however, nothing strains a friendship more than living together, so sometimes it is a good idea to think about allowing yourself some space, unless these friends will respect your needs fully.

The summer before you start

'School is finished, you have completed your last exam and you are waiting for your results to find out where you are going. If you have been lucky enough to receive an unconditional acceptance to university or college, visit the university again. Email the administrator for your course and ask if they could send you the module handout. Some universities will provide this which tells you if there is a mandatory textbook and what the reading will be. I did this when I went to university and found that it gave me something to focus on during the summer holidays as well as helped me feel more prepared. Finally, and possibly one of the more important tasks to do is to contact student services and ask what the procedure is for gaining support. The chances are you will need to complete a form and wait on an appointment which is normal, but you will have a head start to others.

Sarah Gardiner, *Autistic student*

The summer between the end of sixth form/college is potentially the longest time you will ever have without assignments or a full-time job for a very long time. Say you finish your exams in May or June, that can mean you have anything between two and a half and four months off, so having a plan is a good idea.

Some popular things for students to do during the summer include travelling (specifically interrailing given our close proximity to Europe), volunteering or getting a job. I did the latter, and it was perfect for me as it kept me busy, active, and meant I was saving money for university. However, everyone is different and will have different goals for their long summer. If you have friends to travel with, this can be a great time to see parts of the world and experience other cultures. However, being with other people 24/7 comes with its own challenges for Autistic people, and therefore scheduling in time to unwind and 'de-social' is essential when travelling.

What many Autistic people find is that they are incredibly burnt out after their A-Levels, and indeed the last 14 years of full-time schooling; therefore, for many, a long rest is in order. This is perfectly natural, and taking this time to recuperate will ensure you are ready for university in the autumn.

Make a list of things you would like to do, give yourself lots of time to do them, and remember that you have achieved so much to get to this point in your life, you are now in control of your time and what you do with it.

The transition from school to university

This is a big change, there is no denying that. It may be the biggest change you will have experienced up to this point. However, that does not mean it is unmanageable, or that you will not thrive through it. You have got to the point where you have a place at university, and the next step is to prepare yourself to manage the transition from school to starting your degree.

Small changes can help manage this. If you don't already, consider cooking dinner for yourself more often in the lead-up to moving away, and do your own laundry (tempting as it is to let someone else manage all that!). University means more independence, and your feet may be itching to jump into this new world, but it can also be overwhelming when it all comes at you at once. Taking small steps to increase your independence before moving away can help you. If you are staying at home while studying for your degree, consider how you will manage your environment to best increase your success. Do you find you can work in your bedroom, or is there a library nearby you can work from if you do not want to go onto the university campus? If you are doing an online degree, make sure you have an ergonomic set-up and plenty of space to work from.

Preparing to transition begins while you are at school/college, however, as you are leaving behind a large part of your education as you move on up to higher education, take time to consider this and to speak to your teachers about what this means for you. Read below about Sophia's experience of preparing to transition to university and the steps she took to make this easier.

'Going to secondary school can be a scary experience for some children, but as an undiagnosed Autistic child, I found the move particularly challenging. I experienced extremely high levels of anxiety and would often refuse to go to school, though, at the time, I couldn't articulate why. I now know that I found the environment overwhelming. The various sounds, the crowded corridors, and the unexpected timetable changes were all contributing factors. When I did manage to get into school, I would 'mask' these difficulties. I was quiet and reserved and tried hard to blend into the background. Despite the challenges I experienced in school, I loved learning and enjoyed the routine school provided. I was one of few students who liked having a school uniform as it was the same every day and provided me with some much-needed consistency!

I received my Autism diagnosis aged 16 – just before the start of my A-Levels. At the time, the thought of leaving school and attending university seemed impossible! I was finally beginning to understand myself, as were the people around me. I couldn't cope with the thought of another transition; I didn't think I could manage it. I was happy to stay where I was, surrounded by familiar faces, and had hoped to get a job there as a Teaching Assistant in the SEN department.

My family and my teachers, however, had other ideas. They believed I would thrive at university, so the planning began to get me there. We had two years of Sixth Form to prepare for it.

We started by discussing some of the most important things to me. They were:

1. I wanted to be within travelling distance of home
   (I certainly wasn't ready to live on campus!)

and

2. If I was going to go to university, I wanted to study psychology.

The fear of leaving school and delving into uncertainty was still intense, but the school's SENCo (Special Educational Needs Coordinator) suggested an excellent idea. We went around the school and took photos of all my favourite places and the staff, and some of my teachers wrote me letters. We put these into an album for me to look at whenever I missed school. I still have this today, →

and taking photos of places that make me feel safe has become one of my coping strategies. And so, after many months of preparation, the time had finally come for me to leave school and move on to university – and the support did not stop there. My teachers remained in contact with me and the university until I built new relationships and was ready to advocate for myself.

I didn't realise after my diagnosis how important it was to find out that I'm Autistic when I did, but looking back, that knowledge, combined with the support of my family and some very special teachers, helped me to transition to university and continue my education – something I am so glad that I did.

Sophia Christophi, *Autistic psychology student*

Consider taking photos of your school/college like Sophia did, and keep in contact with your teachers if you can. You could also bring in a small notebook and ask teachers to write in it for you, like the letters Sophia's teachers wrote her. Meaningful memory-making like this can help you have a nice memento to keep, but also make it a smoother transition, rather than an abrupt end on results day before you leave for university.

Academically, it is also a big change. Have a read of the tips in Chapter 7, and see if you can implement some of these before you start, such as developing a timetable for catching up on lecture notes. Of course, you might not get your timetable in advance, in which case focus on getting any summer reading done and making sure you have rested enough to be prepared.

Chapter 3: Arriving

My advice to all Autistic students would be to see if you can arrive on campus a few days early. Many universities will offer this, but even if they don't, you can send an email to ask. Most universities will have two arrival dates: one for international students, and one for home students. If you email ahead of arriving, you may be able to arrive with the international students. Arriving early allows you to get your bearings, settle in, and explore the spaces before the campus becomes too busy with all the other new students. From things like getting to choose which kitchen cupboards work best for you, to finding the student support offices and local shops, arriving early can help you a lot as an Autistic student. Some universities even offer special settling-in activities for Autistic students during this time, with meet-and-greets with other Autistic students across different years, and getting to explore the quieter campus together. In August, contact the student support team, or disability support service, at the university, and send them an email to ask about what is available to you – the template below might help.

Example email:

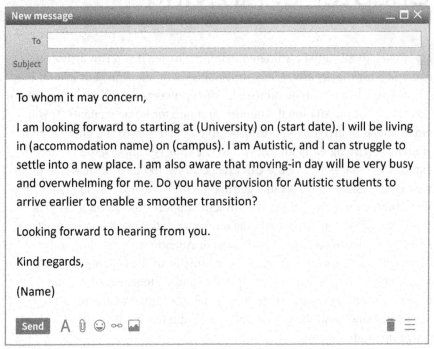

New message   _ □ ×

To

Subject

To whom it may concern,

I am looking forward to starting at (University) on (start date). I will be living in (accommodation name) on (campus). I am Autistic, and I can struggle to settle into a new place. I am also aware that moving-in day will be very busy and overwhelming for me. Do you have provision for Autistic students to arrive earlier to enable a smoother transition?

Looking forward to hearing from you.

Kind regards,

(Name)

Send   A 📎 ☺ ∞ 🖼   🗑 ≡

What to pack?

Everything probably needs to fit in a car, so it helps to know what to pack. Some of you will need to fit everything in a suitcase or two to take on a train. In these cases, it is best to wait until you are in your new city to buy bedding and kitchen supplies, as you will need the space in your suitcase for clothes. Below are some ideas of things you might want to consider taking, and not taking, to university. Of course, everyone is different, and your own list will depend on what kind of accommodation you are moving into. If you are staying at home for university, feel free to skip this section, although you may find parts useful for things to purchase before you start your course. You'll find these sections in list form at the end of the book, where you can tick them off once you've packed them.

Laptop

A laptop is the best purchase you can make before starting university. They are expensive, however, and not everyone can afford one, so look into disability grants and funding if you need to, because a laptop that will last you throughout your degree is going to be incredibly useful. Some

universities will give you access to everything you need in terms of software, so you can skip buying an Office package (Word, Excel, PowerPoint etc.) as they will provide this. The same goes for any packages you need for your degree, such as MATLAB or SPSS, although many universities will use software such as 'R' that you can download for free. (If you don't know what I'm talking about here don't worry – these tend to be for mathematics and computing subjects!) If you can't afford a laptop, and don't have DSA that will pay for it, the library often will have laptops that can be loaned out, so it's worth getting in there early at the start of the year.

Warm clothes

When packing clothes, remember you are packing for the next term, it could be 25 degrees when you move in in September, but it can get down to negative numbers in the winter, so warm coats, layers, hats, scarves and gloves are a must. If you have trouble regulating your body temperature, warm layers that are easily removed are ideal – try snapping up a university-branded hoodie when you arrive, many people live in these for three years. Pack enough clothes that you only need to do a wash once a week, think 14 pairs of underwear, at least ten tops, and four or five pairs of bottoms at a minimum.

Toiletries

Toilet roll probably isn't top of your list of things to remember, but you might find, after a long drive to your university halls, that you or someone you've come with needs to use your brand-new bathroom, only to find there are no supplies, so come prepared! Make sure to bring some hand soap too, and if there are certain products you like to use, or you have sensitive skin, bring them with you as it might take you a while to find where they sell them in your new town. Remember to pack two of things like towels, as you will be changing them regularly, and one will probably always be in the wash. Pack two big towels and two hand towels, and at least one bathmat if they are not provided, you might need to bring extra towels if you have long hair like me and need to put it up! If you can stretch to it, a towelling robe is a fantastic thing to own; you don't need to worry about it slipping off, so you have your hands free, it can have pockets, and you will be much cosier.

When packing toiletries, consider bringing a pack of condoms and some lube. Even if you are not sexually active and don't plan to be, it can be helpful if a friend needs a condom to be able to give them a couple. You can get condoms for free at sexual health clinics, from your school nurse, or through schemes such as the C-Card, so you shouldn't need to buy any. When carrying condoms, make sure to carry them in a secure container, so they don't get ripped by keys. Condom companies sell small metal tubs that can fit in your wallet and can hold three or four condoms at a time.

Bedding, boots, bags, books

You will also need bedding. Some universities will let you buy a bedding pack when you arrive, or you can bring your own. They won't usually provide sheets though, so bring at least two sets of sheets with you. Make sure to consider that it may be warm when you arrive, but it certainly won't be in two- or three-months' time, so bring a blanket or thick duvet as well.

On the topic of it being cold, a pair of boots, or shoes with a good grip, are essential for everyone who is off to university. You will likely be doing a lot of walking once you start university, and the icy ground can be deadly in the winter months, and trainers might not cut it. A pair of walking boots or similar will allow you to get to lectures on time without a twisted ankle!

Along with the walking, you'll also need to carry everything you need for lectures around with you. Make sure you get a good strong backpack that can hold your laptop and books in it. This will also come in useful when you go food shopping too, as it is much better to carry stuff on your back than hurting your hands with multiple bags. Also consider bringing a small bag with you for nights out. I always liked having a bum bag that could go around my waist; it meant I had my hands free so I could dance, and I also didn't have to worry about it falling off my shoulder. It is also harder for someone to try to steal a bag if it is literally attached to you.

Books are heavy, but to many they are a necessity. Buying textbooks for your course can help you prepare for the content, as well as avoid trying to borrow them from the library. Bring some books to read for pleasure too, a mixture of ones you might want to reread, and those you have been wanting to read for a while. Keeping up with reading for pleasure is so important while at university, as it is often easy to end up just reading for your course. For reading these books, maybe bring a reading light or lamp, as not all accommodations have these.

Laundry supplies

A laundry bag or basket is a good thing to have with you, particularly one that is easy to carry to the laundry room and back. If you are allowed to dry your clothes in your room (some universities don't allow this as it increases the humidity and can lead to mould) you'll need a clothes airer. If you will be drying most things, but need an airer for a few items that can't go in the dryer like bras and period underwear, consider getting a small airer that goes over the radiator, which can save space and clothes dry much more quickly! Bring laundry detergent and fabric conditioner if the machines are not self-dosing, or if you have sensitive skin, or you if just prefer a certain brand.

Stationery

If you are a stationery lover like me, you might find that brand-new supplies for university help to hype you up for your new course. It might also help you to separate mentally between A-Levels and degree-level study if you have new sets for your new environment. I brought a new folder for each of my six modules and a new notepad. A very useful item I bought once at uni was a printer – it was £40 and still works to this day! I would wait until you are at university to buy any larger items like this, however, as you may find printing is cheaper than buying a printer.

Décor

It's always a good idea to bring some things that remind you of home, some pictures, cuddly toys, or posters you had up in your room. Most places won't allow you to put posters up as they can mark the walls, however, there are some non-marking adhesives out on the market now which can help to get around this, but check the rules of your accommodation before putting anything up!

Mattress protector

Some universities provide a mattress protector for all students, but if they don't it's a good idea to bring one, not just because you don't know how many times the mattress has been used, but it also protects you somewhat if you end up spilling coffee all over the bed!

Kitchenware

You'll need less kitchen stuff than you think, as most things can be washed up and reused within one cooking session. Having less cooking stuff also means you stay on top of your washing up, which can not only ingratiate you to your housemates but also help your mental health (trust me!). You'll need a mug and a glass – consider a nice big mug, as you can then have cup-a-soup and mug brownies (recipe at the end of the book) in them. One large plate, one small plate, one cereal bowl and one pasta bowl should be all you need – this will see you through a day without needing to wash up after each meal. Two sets of cutlery (knife, spoon, teaspoon, and fork), some sharp knives, a spatula, and two wooden spoons are also musts. Bring at least three tea towels – try and get funky ones, and this goes for all your kitchenware: the more different it is from everybody else's, the less likely it will accidentally end up in someone else's drawer or cupboard. I chose a colour scheme and made sure all my plates and cutlery were that colour, so if there was a random unclaimed fork, I knew it wasn't mine. For washing up, you'll also need sponges and washing-up liquid. Also bring a kitchen spray to clean down surfaces with after you've finished cooking. If you have sensitive skin or don't like the feel of washing up, bring some gloves to wear.

Two pans will probably be enough for cooking, one high-sided one for boiling veg and pasta, and one for frying and stir-fries. A sieve will function as a colander as well, so no need to buy both. Bring a baking tray big enough for a pizza, and two chopping boards (one for meat, one for veg). For storing food, bring sandwich bags and some Tupperware, and remember to bring or buy cling film, kitchen foil and baking paper. A reminder here not to put kitchen foil in the microwave: it will catch fire!

What you don't need to pack

You might be tempted to take everything you own to university with you, however this can make your room feel cluttered, leading you to feel overwhelmed. You will also accumulate more stuff over the year, so if the car is stuffed full when you arrive, you'll need two trips on the way back! Pack light, and prioritise the essentials and things that will make you feel at home. There are some things you definitely don't need to take.

Iron

The number one pair of items I repeatedly see unpacked from the backs of cars on move-in day are an iron and ironing board. Now, if you often wear shirts you have ironed yourself, or are doing a vocational degree like medicine or teacher training where you need to dress in smart shirts, sure, bring them. Otherwise, I can guarantee that thing will never get used. People pack them with good intentions, or because their parents use them to iron their school shirts. Let me tell you something: once you start university, the last thing you will be doing is ironing. Save your money and buy extra hangers, you will always need more of them.

Summer clothes

You also do not need to pack your summer wardrobe when you start in September/October. Unless you are moving out of where you currently live permanently, see if you can leave some clothes there. The same goes for your winter clothes in the third term, no point having items you are not going to use cluttering up your room.

Cooking appliances

In terms of your kitchen, check beforehand, but the majority of self-catered halls will already have a kettle, microwave and toaster. You don't need to bring your own, and any extras like a toastie-maker, waffle iron, or fondue station are also most likely going to collect dust. Bring the essentials, and then if you find out in your fourth week that you desperately need an avocado peeler, you can get one then.

A car

Now this one comes with quite a few caveats: you may require a car for access, for support, or even for your course. However, if none of these are the case, don't bring your wheels to university. There is unlikely to be anywhere to park, and universities are usually laid out so that you don't need one. For my undergraduate degree, a car was essential because I needed to drive to my teaching placements, sometimes up to an hour away, where there was no public transport available. However, for my master's, my car gathered dust as every lecture was within walking distance and there would not have been anywhere to park had I even wanted to drive there.

Gaming chairs

This might be a controversial one. As someone who is not an avid gamer myself, I never understood those who lugged a heavy chair up four flights of stairs into their student room. It is a very bulky item, which likely won't fit in the average car. While gaming is fun, see how you do without the chair, the TV screen, and all the additions, before committing to a large item in what will probably be a small room. However, this may be an essential to you, which is also okay, just check the university's policy on bringing furniture into the room.

Hot plates, kettles, rice cookers, minifridges, and heaters

These are non-essentials mainly because the university will likely confiscate them. Most universities require electrical items such as these to be tested, and they are highly regulated, for example if anything without a UK plug will normally not be allowed. Avoid having your items taken off you, and don't pack these. You can sometimes get exemptions for fridges in your room if you need to keep medication in them – contact the university in advance to discuss this as they will need to do an electrical test on anything like that that you bring.

Mature students

A mature student is defined as anyone over the age of 21 at the time they start their undergraduate degree. This is something of an arbitrary definition, as for student finance purposes you are not considered an independent student until the age of 25. However, there is a big difference between an 18-year-old straight out of school and someone who has been working and living independently for a few years before they start their course. Many mature students start university in middle-age, or even once they have retired. While this book is primarily aimed at those starting university from school or college, hopefully you can gain something from the advice from Luce below.

'To thine own self be true and this has gone both ways for me. Congratulations, you're back in academia! You come with a real-world perspective that is valuable – you probably also have a stronger identity and awareness of your strengths, and also challenges. This awareness can be leveraged to help you in your studies. For myself, my tasks this year have been learning how to exist in the classroom, with its social dynamic, and forming new patterns of schedule and self-care from previous ones. I have been learning how to deal with my reactions to the new environment, how to work in academia, trying to learn how to be kind to myself, but to be aware of what's happening most of all. This has helped me form mechanisms for promoting my strengths and supporting my deficits, too.

Working with younger people has been frustrating beyond compare. The priorities are simply not the same, as are experiences and interests. ➔

As someone who was diagnosed at 44, I suffered being the social outcast my whole life, learning how to exist in the world. Then I learned the explanation for decades of painful experiences and started building ways to healthfully cope. Maybe you've gone through the same story. Being back in a classroom has brought those experiences back, and it has been hard.

I remind myself that they have "learner's eyes". How can you use this perspective to help yourself?

Seek out people in the same situation if possible. You can do this on campus or through social media. They are more likely to have the same, if not neurotype, but a more complex understanding of the world and also similar motivations for being a student. I've joined social media networks of NDs [neurodivergent people] that have been helpful both emotionally and academically.

Allow yourself to vent (responsibly, of course), without guilt. One bonus of many academic programmes is support systems like accommodations and therapy and tutoring services – take advantage of them! I also have consciously made time for my personal pursuits and maintaining my previous social network. Make sure to allocate time for your physical health – exercise promotes cognition and retention! Otherwise, I have found I devote all my time to my studies relentlessly and then wonder why I am suffering from symptoms of breakdown.

Be kind to them, but also to yourself.

Luce, *Autistic applied linguistics student*

The intersection of being both a mature student and Autistic may make you feel more isolated at first, but as Luce says, finding other people in your situation is very important. Sharing similar experiences with those at the same point in life as you can be very valuable and help you realise there is no right or wrong time to go to university. Yes, most of the undergraduate students will be under 21, but there is no time limit on receiving an education, and your added experience and skills will be an asset to you and your peers. Once you have been there for a year or two, the differences between yourself and younger peers will become fewer, as they learn to live independently for the first time and mature into young adults.

Registering at a GP

It is essential to register with a GP as soon as possible when you arrive at university, don't wait until the first time you are ill. A common concern many students have is that they won't be able to access the doctors when they are back home for the holidays. However, you can use *any GP surgery* as a temporary patient for up to three months at a time. So, register permanently with one near your university. There might be a choice of GPs – see which one the university recommends, which one is closest to you, and even ask the students union (SU) which one they would recommend. Mostly all will offer the same services, but sometimes one will have a reputation for being particularly good for, for example, LGBTQ + students, people with long-term conditions such as chronic fatigue syndrome, or students with mental health difficulties.

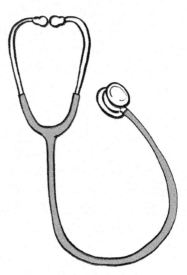

Considerations for LGBTQ+ students

Look at the SU website for your university, or email their welfare officer directly. For example, it might be worth asking whether a particular GP surgery has a reputation for being particularly welcoming of transgender students. Of course, every NHS practice should offer the same level of care, but it is worth chatting to other LGBTQ + students about their experiences of accessing specialist services.

Vaccinations

Ironically, I write this chapter with a positive lateral flow test (LFT) sitting beside me. I lasted three years without catching it, but Covid finally got me, and this has been a lesson to me that no matter how healthy we might think we are, or how much green tea we drink, none of us are invulnerable to illness. Never is this truer than when you start university. Remember how quickly Coronavirus spread across the globe? Now imagine 60 more viruses, among people from all over the UK, all over the globe, all coming together in a one-mile radius and sharing the same bars, lecture rooms and offices. This is not meant to scare, but to bring forward the reality of what is necessary to safeguard your health as this new chapter of your life begins.

Some things are unavoidable, but that does not mean you shouldn't be prepared! First things first: get all your vaccinations. You can request your vaccination record from your GP – if you are born in the UK, this will list all the vaccinations you should have had, and which ones you *did* have. Some could have been missed due to illness, miscommunication or being away/under lockdown at the time. Contact your GP early on to request any you have missed, as some cannot be taken together, so you might need to spread them out over a few months.

I was lucky enough to have been in the first year of recipients of the HPV vaccine in 2008, and since then they have improved it to cover more strains, reduced it to two vaccines, and begun offering it to men. HPV (human papillomavirus) is incredibly common, with about 80% of people becoming infected at some time in their lives. It is transmitted through touch (verruca, warts etc.) or sexual contact (any form of touching the genital area). There are over 150 different strains (types), and many strains are not anything to worry about, resolve on their own, and cause no problems. However, there are some problematic strains that can cause inconvenient and uncomfortable things like genital warts, or that can be deadly like cancers of the cervix, throat or anus. These are the ones the vaccine will help protect against. Even if you are not sexually active, or think you will never be sexually active, it is recommended to get these vaccines before starting university. The worst that can happen is you'll be protected against something you don't come into contact with. **The best that can happen is it could save your life**.

Next up is the flu. It happens every year without fail and can be pretty nasty, even if you're 18, fit, and healthy. Some universities or towns offer university students a flu vaccination for free, but even if they don't, they are normally around £10-£15 at pharmacies. Not everyone can afford this of course, but for me, £10 is close to how much one would spend on lemon and honey tea, tissues, vapour rub, throat sweets and paracetamol, not to mention the hours lost from work being poorly in bed. Arguably a worthy investment, and you have the added benefit of protecting those around you too.

Vaccines are essential, and you should not start university without protection. I have seen some people appear fairly blasé about illness, taking selfies with their mumps, or throwing Covid parties to gain immunity. To this, I say you can never anticipate how you will react to an illness. I have known perfectly healthy 20-year-olds develop debilitating long-Covid, seen people enter intensive care with meningitis (see p.178), and know of men who suffered unwanted infertility after catching mumps: these things are not trivial. Check with your doctor, get vaccinated.

Note: Not everyone can have every vaccine – you might have an allergy to some of the ingredients, or have a condition that means you cannot receive immunisations. This makes it even more important for those that can get the vaccines to take up the opportunity.

Freshers' week/induction week

The first week at university for first-year students is often called 'freshers' week' and is a chance to get to grips with the university environment before the other students arrive. It is a great time to meet new people, make friends, and learn where everything is before lectures start.

> **Freshers' fair:** A gathering of clubs, societies and student groups in one place. There are often stalls for each group and freebies on offer. Some companies may also be there, such as employers or the local gym.

There is a reputation for freshers' weeks to include heavy drinking and lots of parties, however while this may be the case for some people, universities are increasingly trying to move away from this perception and include activities that do not include alcohol, as well as lots of opportunities to meet staff in your department and look round places such as the library and gym facilities. Many universities have rebranded the first week as an 'induction week', or similar names, to move away from the perceptions of alcohol-fuelled mayhem portrayed in films and media. Your freshers' week is what you make it, and if your only goal is to find your way around the university and to get to know your flatmates, do not pressure yourself into attending every event possible, as it is likely you will become burnt out before the term even starts, as Sophie details below.

Fresher's week brought about a multitude of emotions and experiences for me. Like many Autistic students, the hype surrounding freshers' week can induce a particular kind of anxiety, starting weeks before as a distant hum, becoming louder and harder to push away as the week approaches. Before I arrived the thought of meeting my new flatmates was terrifying, but what I hadn't anticipated was the constant and debilitating FOMO that I felt over the course of the week. I was so anxious to bond with my flatmates and dreaded being perceived as the "weird", introverted kid all over again. Certain events that they were going to were my idea of hell; things like a "UV Light Party" would have been a sensory nightmare for me.

Despite my spiralling anxieties around my flatmate's approval, one night in was not enough to destroy the friendships we'd formed in the course of a few days. What fresher's week taught me is that my own method of forced perseverance and going out to events that made me deeply uncomfortable was not worth it in the slightest. Subsequently, I started my first term utterly exhausted, ill and burnt out. While this is a shared experience for many freshers, most people are able to gradually recover in the days following. However, for Autistic students, this is not the case. →

If I were to do fresher's week again, I would choose to attend the day events and activities and to take things at my own pace. The myths that are propagated surrounding the whole concept of fresher's often elevate its status into something unrealistic. In actuality, it is merely a week at the start of term and rarely has long-lasting consequences on your university experience.

Sophie Taylor-Davies, *Autistic English literature student*

Freshers' week is a busy and often over-stimulating time, so make sure you take time for yourself to pause and relax among all the newness, eat well, and get lots of sleep. Arriving at university a few days before all the other new students will also help with this time.

However, you may be the kind of person who cannot wait to attend as many parties as possible. I discovered during my freshers' week that nightclubs were surprisingly fun, and I loved singing, dancing and having fun with the new people I had met. University is a time to try new things, and you never know, you might surprise yourself.

Freshers flu

Freshers' flu is the inevitable cold-like symptoms that begin to occur among new students any time from the first week they arrive to the end of the first term. Of course, not everyone will succumb to these symptoms, but many do. The 'flu' (it is usually not as serious as actual flu) is a bad cold that is the result of your body being around a whole host of new viruses. Everyone who starts at university (unless they are your identical sibling!) will be coming from a slightly different environment, with a different body full of germs, and all these people coming together at once is a recipe for illness. However, there are things you can do to protect yourself and others; you can obviously wear a mask

and sanitise your hands regularly to stop germs from being passed on, but you can also do things to make sure your body can fight off illnesses, such as eating healthily and reducing stress.

Overall, it may not be possible to stop yourself from getting freshers' flu, but the more you look after yourself, the quicker you might recover.

Your first lecture and seminar

> **Lecture:** A class where an educator, a lecturer, talks to large group of students about a topic.

Lectures tend to take place in large auditoriums and will sometimes have up to 400 people in one lecture, although some smaller degree courses will hold lectures in classrooms. Make sure you arrive early as this helps you get the best seat (for me, this was with nobody behind me and at the end of a row). The lecturer will introduce themselves; this is important to note down, as most academics and higher education staff in the UK go by their first names, e.g., 'Hi I'm Joan and I'll be your theoretical physics module one leader'. However, some go by their professional titles, for example, 'Hi I'm Doctor/Professor Smith'. As with anyone's pronouns and choice of name, it is important to respect this and use whatever title they introduce themselves as. If in doubt, ask, or check your emails to see what they sign themselves off as!

Start of you mean to go on: if you want to keep meticulous written notes, bring a fresh notepad and a few pens. If you want to type, bring your tablet or laptop. And if you want to just listen, and then make notes to the recording later, be prepared for that (be aware that even after the pandemic, recordings are not 100% reliable, so making notes is recommended, in case of technical difficulties).

After the lecture, write down the key things you learned, and any references or further reading you want to do around the subject. I would often put a star next to things I needed to research further, and then highlight them once I had done so.

> **Seminar:** A class with a small group of students where discussions and activities take place. Sometimes called a tutorial.

Seminars are different from lectures and are more like the lessons you will have had at school. They are usually led by one of the lecturers, or by a teaching assistant, often a PhD student in that department. This is your chance to go over what was said in the lectures, have discussions, practise questions, or do group projects. They are more informal than lectures, where usually one person talks for an hour (although they may ask questions to the audience). There might also be practical activities, where you learn how to use some software in an IT room, or do experiments in a laboratory. This is where you will likely get given assignments, although they are sometimes given in lectures, and it is a good place to ask questions if you are struggling.

Your first meeting with your tutor

> **Personal tutor:** An academic you meet with regularly to discuss your progress and any issues you might be having. Sometimes called an academic advisor. Not all universities offer this.

Some universities also have **personal tutors**, or academic advisers, who are like mentors in academia. You will usually meet with them one-on-one, and they are a great resource, as staff are incredibly busy at university, and this individual support is invaluable. They can be good for asking questions about staying on track, academic conventions, and your progress in general. Say you are struggling to decide your modules for your third year, you want help with developing a master's application, or you are unsure whether to reference things lecturers say in lectures in your essays, they can usually help with these things. Make sure you attend your first meeting, giving a good impression is important as you may have this relationship with this academic for a few years. Make a list of questions in advance, and think before you go in about what you would like to get out of having an academic adviser. Not all universities have an individual person assigned to every student, however, they will all have some form of academic support available where you can discuss things one-to-one with someone.

Your first trip to the library

Getting your library card (often also your ID card for the whole time you're at university) is probably the first time you'll go to the library. I was both over and underwhelmed when I first entered the library. Overwhelmed because of the size, I had never seen so many books in one place, and they all looked really interesting. Underwhelmed because there wasn't a single fiction novel anywhere to be seen.

University libraries are different from school libraries in that they primarily hold course texts and books around the course subjects. Some will also have archives, and old book collections for those studying history or archaeology. They won't tend to have anything you would consider reading for pleasure, for that you would need to get a library card for the local, non-university library. The libraries often have a multitude of study spaces, and it can be difficult to navigate these. For example, there might be one floor or space dedicated to group work, and people are likely to be chatting here, and there will be a silent study area where those who rustle pages too loudly get given dirty stares. And there is sometimes an area where you can study and eat or drink, although this is sometimes banned altogether.

Library etiquette demands that you can take short breaks outside of your study area, but not 'seat hog' where you leave your belongings at a study space or computer, to not return for a few hours. I always enjoyed spending time in the library, as it was a peaceful place, and the group areas were a good place to catch up with people. Working silently alongside others helped me fulfil my social needs for the day, while not burning myself out.

Navigating the laundry room

After being at university for a week, you will start to realise something: you are now in charge of your own washing. You may have done this yourself before you went to university, but if you, like the majority of young people who start university, had a parent or guardian do the majority of your laundry, this will be a new experience. When you move in, you'll be told where the laundry room is and how to pay for your washing. This is normally by pre-paid card these days, but can also be by coins, or online systems.

With prices steadily rising to eye-watering levels, you may not have the luxury of doing whites and darks loads, so if you want to keep your clothes close to their original colours, colour-catching sheets can help with this – although I never used them, I just let my whites get slowly pinker over the years.

Many machines are self-dosing these days, which means you do not need to buy washing liquid and fabric conditioner. However, check this in advance. Additionally, if you have sensitive skin or allergies, it is best to use the non-self-dosing machine to avoid a reaction.

In my experience, there are never enough machines for the number of students. I always did my washing late at night when it was quiet. This also reduces the likelihood your newly washed clothes will be taken out of the machine by an impatient person wanting their turn. In case this does happen, I recommend buying a few laundry bags; they keep all your washing together, and they have smaller bags which are good for bras. This will stop the bra hooks from damaging the rest of your clothes. If you don't have laundry bags, sticking your bras into a pillowcase will work just as well.

You are often not allowed to dry your clothes in your room in case mould starts growing due to the humidity it causes, so using the university dryers may be the only option. However, some items, such as bras and period pants, should not be put in the dryer, so it is best to dry these in your bathroom if you can. Items will normally say 'do not tumble dry' on the label. You should avoid taking anything that says 'dry clean only' to university.

The laundry room can be an anxious place to be: the machines are loud and there can be lots of people there. Finding a time to go when it is quiet and less busy can help you navigate this. Going at the same time every week can also help to develop a routine. My time for laundry was about 10pm on a Monday, and I was often the only person there at this time. I would leave my washing for a few hours while I went to my room and tidied a bit, then come back, put it all in the dryer, and read a book for the 30 minutes that it took to finish. Having those hours to myself to do this self-care task always made me feel calm and like I was taking control of my life.

If you find the laundry room at your university too difficult to navigate due to sensory challenges, there are often laundry services in cities and towns you can try, although the hours for these will vary to your university's services, so it's worth checking before you set off.

One important thing is to wash things regularly. You shouldn't use a towel for more than a week, and bedsheets should be changed *at least* every two weeks, preferably weekly. Having fresh, clean clothes and bedding will help not only with being hygienic but also with your mental health.

Chapter 4: Looking after yourself

When you start at university, the priority is not always 'how can I be the best I can be?', but often 'how can I get through this week?' It's a different environment, with new people, different expectations, and a whole new set of freedoms and responsibilities you have not encountered before. Therefore, the priority is making sure you get through each day, stay healthy, and can get to a point where you are settled and happy. As an Autistic person, the transition to this point may take longer than for others, and therefore acknowledging this and allowing yourself more time to take care of yourself is the best thing you can do when you start at university.

Physical health

Eat five portions of fresh fruit and vegetables a day in three evenly spaced meals with healthy greens as snacks in between, drink lots of water and exercise vigorously for 30 minutes a day. Easy, done, next chapter, right?

No.

While these goals are great, and there is research to support how these all help to maintain a healthy body and lifestyle, sometimes goals like this set us up to fail, and just aren't sustainable every day. I find that, as an Autistic person, I am often more sensitive to 'failure' when it comes to rules about what one should be doing and eating, and when, and how much. It is important to take a step back, listen to your body and think:

what do I need? Learning how to read your body is tricky for anyone, but there is evidence that Autistic people especially struggle to read the signals their body is giving them. Safe foods are called that for a reason, and if your body is telling you that, after a day of lectures and walking home in the rain, you want chopped-up hotdogs in ketchup on potato waffles, that might well be exactly what you need. Likewise, if your body is telling you to get the bus to the shops rather than walk, it might be for a reason, it is preventing you from getting tired or burnt out. For a quick physical health checklist, see the resources section at the back of the book.

Food

Whatever your relationship with food currently is, it will likely change if you move into university accommodation. For many people, this is the first time they will cook exclusively for themselves, the first time they are wholly responsible for cleaning up the kitchen area, and the first time they are sharing a kitchen space and fridge with people they are not related to. Or you may be in catered accommodation, and this is the first time you must leave your living area for each of your meals, to sit in a large room with everyone else eating their meals. It can be a big change.

THEY SAID I NEEDED MORE IRON

Importantly, you need to make sure you are getting enough iron. Iron can be found naturally in red meat and in dark-green leafy vegetables like kale. Lack of iron, or iron deficiency – anaemia – can lead to lack of energy, heart palpitations and shortness of breath. Many young people, especially people who menstruate, are actually iron deficient, and it is hard to get enough iron into your diet, particularly if you don't eat red meat. Multivitamins that contain iron can be a good solution to this and can be bought relatively cheaply. Always check with your doctor before taking anything.

For those days when you don't feel like cooking, it helps to be prepared so you don't end up blowing your whole budget on takeaways. Buy a big bag of onions and when you have the spoons, dice them and put a portion in each of a couple of freezable food bags. You can do the same with carrots, broccoli, peppers etc. Having these in the freezer means you always have veggies to hand that don't need prep; stick them straight in the pan and you're ready to go. Frozen food can be your friend: you can find cook-from-frozen meat, like sausages, or you can freeze mince to take out the day before you need it. Another good tip is this: when you buy a loaf of bread, stick half in the freezer; you can either defrost it when you need it or stick it straight in the toaster from the freezer.

Here are a couple of staples I found helped me:

Creamy carbonara

You will need:

- Eggs (one per portion)
- Spaghetti
- Chopped bacon/lardons/ meat-free alternative
- Double cream (the smallest tub you can find)
- Frying pan
- Saucepan
- Fork
- Spoon
- Scissors
- Sieve

1. Beat the eggs in a mug and mix in the cream.
2. Boil the spaghetti in water for ten minutes.
3. While the spaghetti boils, fry the bacon (you can cut it up with the scissors straight into the pan).
4. Drain the water from the spaghetti with the sieve.
5. Add the cooked spaghetti to the bacon and stir.
6. Turn off the heat for the hob.
7. Add the eggy cream mixture to the spaghetti and the bacon and stir.
8. Eat straight away. It doesn't taste as good reheated.
9. Wash up as soon as possible.

You can add anything to this, like garlic and onion or broccoli. Chicken carbonara is also nice, just make sure you chop it small and fry it for longer so it isn't pink in the middle. Grated cheese can also be sprinkled on top, or added to the egg mixture.

Bangers and mash

You will need:

- Sausages (the bangers), meat or vegetarian
- Potatoes
- Milk or butter
- An oven tray
- Kitchen foil
- Saucepan
- Chopping board
- Knife
- Potato masher
- Sieve

1. Chop the potatoes into small chunks. The smaller they are, the quicker they will cook. You don't need to peel them unless you really don't like the skins.
2. Boil the potatoes in water.
3. Follow the instructions for oven cooking the sausages. This will involve preheating the oven to a certain temperature and putting the sausages onto the foil and then onto the oven tray.
4. The potatoes are cooked once you can easily cut a chunk in half with a fork. Drain them using the sieve and mash using the masher. Stir in a little milk or butter and serve with the cooked sausages.
5. Wash up.

Optional extras: caramelised onions

- Onions (red or white)
- Sugar
- More butter
- Another saucepan/frying pan
- Spoon

I'm sure there's a special way of doing this but the way I do it is I fry the onions in a load of butter, then turn the heat down and add some sugar. Stir as you go and serve with the sausages and mash.

For sausages, I always use frozen ones and often bought a big bag of 20 to last me a while. This meant I didn't need to worry about them going out of date.

Egg fried rice

You will need:

- Rice
- Eggs (one per portion)
- Mug
- Spoon
- Saucepan
- Sieve
- Frying pan
- Oil
- Peas
- Bowl
- Microwave (optional)
- Soy sauce

1. Boil the rice until cooked, then drain it with the sieve and leave to 'steam dry' for a few minutes, where the water can evaporate off the wet rice.

2. Beat the eggs in a mug.

3. Heat the saucepan with some oil, then add the eggs and stir until they are scrambled.

4. Pop the peas in the bowl with a little bit of water and microwave for 2-3 minutes (or boil in the rice pan if you don't have a microwave).

5. Add the rice to the saucepan and stir so the egg gets mixed in.

6. Add the peas and stir again.

7. Add the soy sauce and fry for 5 minutes, stirring so it's cooked through.

Optional extras:

- Onion
- Cooked prawns
- Peppers
- Spring onion
- Chilli sauce

If adding extra vegetables, take the egg out of the saucepan once you've scrambled it, and cook the vegetables with some oil for a few minutes, then add the egg back in before adding the rice. Cooked prawns should be added to the rice.

A final note on food from my experience of working with undergraduates: kitchen safety cannot be underestimated. You may already know these things, but many do not, so be sure to look out for everyone in your flat too.

Firstly, metal does not go in the microwave, I cannot stress this enough. **Do not** put foil, forks, metal trays, or anything with metal in it, into the microwave. It will catch fire inside the microwave, or worse, blow up.

Secondly, do not put plastic in the oven. We once had an entire block evacuated because someone thought a plastic chopping board was a baking tray and filled his flat with black smoke.

Finally, and most importantly, **do not cook while drunk**. If you have drunk too much to drive, you have drunk too much to cook. Way too many injuries occur because people come home from a night out and try and cook something. When someone has been drinking their reactions and pain tolerances change. This means you might not notice if you are cutting or burning yourself until it is too late. Alcohol also makes people sleepy, and sleep more deeply, meaning they sometimes leave things on a stove or in an oven, which can lead to fires. Have something cold instead, or order a takeaway – and drink some water.

Exercise

You will likely be doing more walking than usual once you start university. Schools tend to be much smaller than universities, and it is not unusual to have to walk for half an hour between buildings or parts of the campus for different things. Factor this in when you think to yourself 'I've not done any exercise this week'. Furthermore, there will be lots of opportunities to get involved with physical activities you haven't experienced before, and the fact that everyone else is new will help with any nerves. Things like Quidditch and water polo which are not on offer in secondary school will introduce you to exercising in a fun way, with other like-minded people. There are also gyms on campus, generally with much cheaper fees than gyms you find outside of universities, and these are a good place to exercise alone as a break from studying and socialising.

Period health

Periods are a topic historically not often talked about, although the (red) tide is changing on this. For people who menstruate, starting university can disrupt your period routine. Stress and a change of environment can impact your cycle, and this can lead to added stress when periods are later, heavier, or missed altogether (amenorrhea). If you experience any abnormal bleeding, or you are worried about your period and your cycle in any way, see a GP as soon as possible.

Tracking your period with an app like Flo can help you not only plan for when your period will arrive, but also spot any irregularities or concerns.

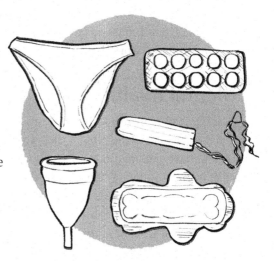

You may also realise you change in the products you use at university, as some people find it hard to maintain usage of reusable products such as cups and period pants in shared bathrooms. Find what works for you in your new environment and be kind to yourself and your body.

Many universities will provide free menstrual products in the toilets and welfare centres, and often they will have boxes you can go to without asking anyone. If you struggle at any point to afford menstrual products, speak to someone like a welfare staff member and they should be able to help you find what you need.

Teeth, eyes and ears

For some reason, teeth and eye care are not always free once you hit a certain age. Check what age this is where you are, and try and make sure you have a dental check-up and eye test before you go to university. If you are worried about your hearing, see if you can get a hearing test too – these are often available at your local opticians.

Sleep

Many Autistic people struggle with sleep, especially those who are also ADHD; sometimes our brains just don't want to let us drift off. Set up your room in a way that is conducive to sleep: dark, cool, no screens. Try and turn off any devices an hour before bed – I know this is hard, but the light from these screens tells your brain it needs to stay awake, so when you then try and get to sleep, it is still confused and tries to keep you up. You can get screen tints that help a little, but the best thing to do is just to turn them off in the lead-up to bedtime. Try not to eat or drink too close to bed either, as if you are still digesting this will keep you up, as will needing to go to the loo. Turn your radiator down or off, and try not to wear too many layers that you overheat in the night. Block out external light by using the blinds and/or an eye mask, and put on a podcast or some music if you need background noise to get to sleep. I always found a drop of lavender oil on my pillow worked wonders for getting me to relax enough to sleep.

Mental health

Positive mental health is vital to your whole life and particularly when you are at university. Being able to face the day, have things to look forward to, and have the emotional energy to interact with others are all signs of positive mental health. Eating a healthy, balanced diet and going outside are more outward signs that things are going well, although this is not always the case. Most students struggle with anxiety, stress, or low mood at some point in their studies, and it is important to notice when things are not right in yourself or others, in order to address them before things get worse. We all have bad days, or bad weeks, but if things are consistently or particularly bad, reach out for help.

Changes in diet and sleep are often the most obvious outward signs that something is amiss; sleeping or eating a lot more or less than usual can be evidence of poor mental health. You might notice this through rapid weight gain or loss – if suddenly your jeans are much looser than you remember, look at your habits to see if anything has changed that might need looking at. Another common sign that someone is struggling is that they stop looking after their body as much as before, this can include things like not showering or brushing their teeth, not wearing clean clothes, or not brushing their hair. If you notice you or someone else has stopped caring for themselves and their appearance, this could be a sign that they are struggling.

Deviations in patterns of socialising are also key to look out for. As Autistic people, we often need time to ourselves to decompress and avoid burnout, but if you find you are avoiding social interactions you used to enjoy or look forward to, this can be a sign of low mood or anxiety. Conversely, acting erratically and doing things you would not normally be comfortable with can also be a sign that something is not right: spending more than usual, having risky sexual encounters or using substances are all things to watch out for as signs of poor mental health. People with low mood and anxiety might not appear so, as their feelings might manifest in different ways such as in anger and lashing out at others. If you find yourself often frustrated, or angry with no reasonable cause, talking to someone about what might be causing it is paramount.

Sometimes people might want a beer or a glass of wine after a hard exam, but if you find yourself or someone else relying on alcohol or another substance, this is a common sign of deteriorating mental health. Alcohol and other drugs can mask feelings, but they do not solve them, and therefore people often feel much worse once the effects of the drug wear off.

It is not always possible to know if someone is struggling – sometimes they are very good at masking their feelings. Checking in on your friends is important, even a quick text can help them realise they are not alone. However, some people might not want you to help them or point out that things might be wrong. If they are not receptive to your helping, do not push it, they might need to work things out for themselves. Try to watch out for the signs of poor mental health in yourself and others to try and maintain positive health and habits. If you are very worried about someone, approach the university support, or even the emergency services, who can support them further.

> **Here's a summary of warning signs to watch out for:**
> - Changes in sleep and eating habits.
> - Not caring for yourself or your appearance.
> - Avoiding social interactions and activities that were previously enjoyed.
> - Risky behaviours.
> - Anger.
> - Substance abuse.

Maintaining your mental health

Keeping yourself healthy, both mentally and physically, is the most important thing you can do at university. You cannot study effectively if you are unwell, and therefore you need to keep on top of the self-care needed to thrive. Autistic people often forget to take self-care measures, as we are at risk of getting caught up in things and people, or taking too much time out for others and forgetting ourselves. This means Autistic people need to take extra care to be aware of their needs and when they need seeing to.

Maintaining your mental health means being present in yourself, and being aware of the emotions and sensations you are feeling. This is especially difficult for Autistic people who can struggle with these aspects. Take time every day to listen to your body, and think: 'Am I hungry?' 'Am I calm?' Going for walks and leaving your room or flat every day will help your mental health, as will cooking food, taking a shower every day, and talking to someone in person or on the phone. Small acts like these can keep you on track to positive thinking:

'Caring for your mental health is vital for Autistic people, particularly those of us living with mental health conditions. Moving to university is often a mental health trigger, but there are ways of managing this. Firstly, register with your new GP practice before you move to university. This is especially important if you take repeat medications, to ensure that you have easy access to your prescriptions. When registering, declare any mental health conditions or difficulties. If you are under a mental health service before attending university, consider transferring your care to your university location. Secondly, register with the university disability service, ideally during the summer before you start. They can put in place both academic and general support for you before the term begins.

I found it helpful to reflect on and identify my own mental health triggers before moving to university so I could plan strategies that I could take with me. During my first year, one of the strategies that I implemented was to regularly spend time away from campus/the university area.

At the start of term, I identified a list of safe spaces that I felt able to go to whenever I felt overwhelmed. Most of these were not near my university, as I needed the distance and security that I would not be surrounded by my peers. Lastly, physical attendance at university is not everything. Your university experience belongs to you and you only. If you are not able to attend everything in person, then that is okay. Take things at your own pace and remind yourself that you have different needs from your peers.'

Sophie Taylor-Davies, *Autistic English literature student*

Here is a summary of tips for maintaining good mental health:
- Leave your room or flat every day.
- Cook a meal.
- Shower daily.
- Go for walks.
- Talk to people.
- Keep a diary.
- Be present, understand what you are feeling.

Burnout

Autistic burnout is a condition resulting from chronic stress and over-exertion without adequate support. It manifests as long-term exhaustion, loss of functioning, and a smaller **window of tolerance**. Burnout can commonly occur due to prolonged **masking**, which, as you enter the highly social environment of university, is likely to occur more often. Reducing how much you mask, and coming out as Autistic, can help you to avoid burnout, although this is not always easy, especially if you have been masking for a long time.

> **Window of tolerance:** The ideal emotional zone between hyperarousal and hypoarousal. In this zone, you can manage life and your emotions effectively.

High levels of stress and overly high expectations can also lead to burnout. Some people feel they are letting their family down if they do not get the grades they expect of them at university, and this adds additional pressure on Autistic people in their new environment.

> **Masking:** To hide, or camouflage, who you are or parts of yourself in order to fit in with those around you.

Not being in an Autistic-friendly environment can lead to Autistic burnout as well, and if you are routinely in very loud, busy and uncomfortable places, your window of tolerance will reduce and you might find yourself less able to cope. Asking for reasonable adjustments might be difficult, especially if you do not want to be treated differently from the other students, but consider asking for what you need in order to prevent yourself from burning out. Consider how someone in a wheelchair would not be thought unreasonable for asking for a ramp to get into the lecture building, and you are perfectly within your rights to ask for the lights to be lowered, or to sit on the end of a row. Being Autistic can be a wonderful thing, but we live in a world that is often not designed for us and we need to take extra care to look after ourselves so we can live as we want to.

'Coping with all of the different aspects of university life can be completely exhausting as an Autistic person, especially as an undergrad or master's student. When you add together regular lectures and seminars, social meet-ups with friends from societies or your classes with the unique pressures of living in halls and the nightmare that is UK public transport… it's a lot.

I've experienced Autistic burnout lots of times over the last decade. Sometimes a few days in a dark room with my hobbies is enough to set it straight and other times it has lasted way longer. I suppose it's a bit of a boom-and-bust cycle. If I'm feeling good, I feel able to take on responsibilities and make exciting plans. If my energy levels then get worn down, I move pretty quickly into a situation where everything is becoming increasingly difficult.

A good example of this would probably be my final year of undergrad. I was doing my degree, volunteering, planning society events and lots more. Burnout creeps in slowly so it started off as finding it a bit harder to do some of my work, and then by the end of the year I was completely exhausted.

It might be helpful to track your energy levels and know your triggers. If you find that going to a lecture and a coffee with friends takes lots of energy, maybe don't head straight to the library afterwards. For me, long English winters are a total killer, so I try and adjust my plans between November and March so that I don't start the New Year a complete exhausted mess.

The one tip that I wish I'd listened to in the earlier stages of my time at university is that there is no shame in taking a break, in saying (to yourself – usually the biggest source of pressure for me is me) actually, I can't work on this essay today and instead I'm going to take a complete rest day. It's way better than pushing yourself. Burnout feels like a deep well and when you're standing at the bottom, reaching the top feels almost impossible. It's better not to fall into it in the first place if you can help it. And if you do get burnt out, know that it will end and you will be okay.

Emma Yeo, *Autistic history student*

As Emma suggests, tracking your energy levels is a good way to spot when you are becoming burnt out. For people who menstruate, period apps often have mood trackers which can be useful for this, or there are also specific mood-tracking apps that are suitable for everyone. Looking out for your own signs and triggers can help you to avoid burnout, and to manage your calendar more effectively so you take care of yourself. You may not be able to do everything you want to, and this can be incredibly frustrating, as if you are being let down by your body. However, remember how far you have come, and how important it is to look after yourself.

Where to get support

The best advice I can give regarding accessing support is to do so as soon as possible. Don't wait until things are really bad to reach out. There are many designated people to help you, as well as organisations, charities and services. You are never alone, no matter what the issue. Finding out where to get support before you need it is very useful, use the resources and organisations at the back of this book to help you develop a list of people and services that can help you.

'Before heading off to university as an Autistic student, the best thing I did was to connect with the team supporting disabled students as early as possible. Depending on where you are going, they might be called something different, but it's usually something like "disability support" or "inclusion". A quick Google of your institution + "disability support" will generally lead you in the right direction. Contact them as soon as possible because these folks will help you with your assessments for disabled students' allowance and support needs. They also tend to be fonts of wisdom for all things inclusion on campus and in the broader university world.

Also, join societies! Although you may never go to any events (like me!), they can be great for meeting people with similar interests. You might be surprised at what you can find on your student union website. You can usually join societies on the website too. Some may have a small administrative cost attached, but most are free to join. The disabled student society is always a good shout to stay on top of any specialised support or signposting you might find helpful.

Becca Selby, *Autistic student in biology with science and society*

Mental and physical health

University is a challenging time, especially for Autistic people, who can face more challenges than many. If you feel your health is deteriorating, contact your GP for an appointment as soon as you can. Additionally, for mental health support, the university will have its own counselling service you can refer yourself to. There are also peer-support groups, and peer welfare officers who can help you access the support you need. In a crisis or emergency, dial 999, or your local crisis team for mental health specifically. If you are not in immediate danger but need advice, call 111 (or visit indirect in Northern Ireland).

Lots of students ask: 'Will they contact my parents/carers?' Currently, unless you have given express permission for them to do so, once you are 18, a university cannot contact your parents or carers, even if they have concerns for your welfare. Therefore, do not worry that anyone back home will know if you approach the university for support, as they are obliged by data protection laws not to disclose it to your family or carers.

Academic support

If you find yourself falling behind on assignments, or struggling to keep up with the workload, speak to your professors first; they want you to pass and will hopefully support you. Other sources of support include academic support offices, which come under different names at different universities, but often provide sessions on study skills, planning assignments and training on using certain software. Often these sessions are in person or online, and you can book onto them quite easily. If you are struggling to find academic support at your university, ask staff in your department, or the students' union for more information.

Legal support

If you have a complaint about your university, your first port of call should be the university itself, and the students' union should be able to help you with this. If, however, it is not resolved internally, you can escalate matters to an ombudsman, which is a person or organisation independent of the university who will look into complaints for free and will be impartial. Find details of the ombudsmen available to students complaining against their university in the resources section of this book (see p.191). These are often used in cases of student expulsion, where the student feels they have been wrongly expelled, or that the disciplinary processes were unfair.

Reasonable adjustments, advocating for yourself

As an Autistic student, you have the right to be able to access your education the same as every other student, and if you need extra support to be able to do this, the university should provide it. Many types of support are accessed through Disabled Student's Allowance (DSA), however, the university also has an obligation to assist you in accessing their services. The term 'reasonable' just means something which is feasible. For example, they could install a ramp for a building so that someone in a wheelchair could access part of it, but wouldn't be expected to knock down and rebuild said building to make it fully accessible. The reasonable adjustment if a whole building is inaccessible would probably be to hold lectures and seminars in a different building.

> **Reasonable adjustments:** Changes made by an organisation to ensure their services are accessible to disabled people.

Common reasonable adjustments for Autistic students are detailed below, but this list is not exhaustive. Have a think about what you need in order to access education to the same extent as non-Autistic students. Your university will likely not offer all these reasonable adjustments, but it is always worth asking about the ones you think you need, as it may be that the university has just never had anyone ask for it before. Apply for DSA alongside requesting reasonable adjustments, as anything the university can't offer might be covered by DSA.

Lectures and seminars:

- Choosing where to sit, such as at the end of a row, or at the back.
- Not being 'cold called' in lectures, where a lecturer picks someone to answer a question who hasn't put their hand up.
- A reduction in background noise in the room, with lower lights if possible.
- Having a clear summary of what the lecture is about and clear notes with easy-to-follow instructions for tasks.
- Longer to complete tasks.
- A clear understanding of when regular fire alarm tests will take place.

Assignments and exams:

- Clear deadlines, with reminders close to hand-in time.
- Being able to give presentations to a smaller audience.
- Extended deadlines when required.
- A smaller, quiet room to take exams in.
- A room to take breaks in during exams.

Accommodation:

- Arriving a few days earlier than other students.
- Being placed in a 'quiet' flat.

- Not to be placed in a shared room, a room with a shared bathroom, or an accommodation where you need to move each term or move out during the holidays.
- As with lecture rooms, a clear understanding of when regular fire alarm tests will take place.
- Being able to live in university halls for the duration of your degree.

General:

- All staff you interact with to be given Autism training.
- Access to an Autistic study skills tutor.
- Extra counselling sessions.
- Help joining or setting up an Autistic peer-support group.
- Extra information before your arrival.
- Having a named contact at the university to discuss any academic or support issues.

Here, Katie talks about the adjustments she had while at university, and what worked and didn't work. Katie advocated for herself when her needs were not being met, but this can sometimes be difficult. Reach out to the disability service, the students' union, or your course rep for support if you need it.

'I contacted the university disability service ahead of time to have adjustments in place before I started. I met with a disability adviser, who explained what adjustments were available, and we discussed which would be most helpful. The adjustments I was given included 25% extra time and a smaller room for exams, and not being penalised for absences. Later, extra time for coursework (one-week extensions) was added, my extra time in exams was increased by 33%, and I was allocated a named contact within my department. Having a named contact has made the most difference, as it has meant there was someone familiar with my course who could keep track of how I was doing, offer advice and support, and help me advocate for myself when necessary.

My adjustments haven't always been implemented properly, such as extra time not being applied, but it's helped to know who I can contact →

(e.g. department disability lead) to resolve issues. In my final year, I became course rep to try to address this, improve awareness and understanding among staff, and better advocate for myself and other disabled students. Although some issues continued, the conversations around accessibility I started led to new adjustments being introduced for assessed presentations.

Katie, *Autistic chemistry student*

Money

When I was about 11, I went into a shop to try and buy some knitting wool (knitting is cool, I'll die on this hill), and my card got declined. The woman said, 'Do you have enough in your account?' I was sure I did because I had checked my balance at the bank (this was before mobile banking!) and it said I had £8 debit. It was a debit card, so I had £8, right? Nope. Credit is money you have; debit is money you are out of. This is confusing because a credit card is where you spend money you don't have, whereas a debit card spends money you do have. Getting your head around money is vital for university, and there will be a lot of new terms, so let's break them down. You might already know a lot of this, so feel free to skim-read this bit – or skip it!

You might have already had a job and an income, or already be on top of your finances. However, this may well be your first time managing your own money, and it can be a bit overwhelming. Here I will explain some things that might help, and we will hear from Stacey about what her experience with money at university was.

Tip 1: Set a budget. This may need to be adapted as the year goes on, but setting limits like 'I don't want to spend more than £50 on food a week, I will keep £10 aside for textbooks' will help you mark out money for certain purposes.

Tip 2: Give yourself pocket money. When your student loan comes in, it will be a large sum of money in one hit. You will feel suddenly very rich – 'Wow! I have £3,000!' No, you don't. You have £3,000 minus rent, spread out over four months. I created a separate bank account where I put this lump sum, and set up a **standing order** to transfer myself £70 a week.

Then, when I looked at my bank account, I would see £35, not the £1,500 I had in total. This stops you from spending more at the start of the term, and leaving yourself with nothing at the end.

> **Standing order:** a regular payment between two bank accounts. It will come out automatically, e.g., on the 15th of every month.

University is expensive. Rent, bills, food shop, doing fun stuff, university equipment. Being Autistic, trying to do these "adult" things can be lots more added stress that can impact studies. I definitely felt that. Unfortunately, I was diagnosed at 21, when I had graduated. I reached out to my GP in my second year because I always knew there was something different about my struggles. My university took my referral as a diagnosis and supported me with a student support plan which was very helpful. I didn't get DSA in the second year as a referral wasn't enough evidence for them. So, I had to buy university equipment myself, I didn't have my own laptop when I started university, and being diagnosed earlier and getting DSA could have helped me with the cost of that.

I definitely recommend applying for DSA as soon as possible, even if you think you won't need it. I will be doing this for my master's.

Finances were always stressful because I was financially independent – my family could not support me. This meant I had to work while doing a full-time bachelor's degree. Sometimes, I would work up to 30 hours a week, just to be able to do what people around me were doing and to actually have savings when I finished my degree. I was always anxious about spending money. Having jobs was extremely stressful, but it meant the financial stress of university throughout my three years was lessened.

But if I had the choice, I would have only worked one day a week, as it can be quite stressful, especially when you are Autistic and most places are understaffed.

Day to day at university I tried to spend as little as possible, I had basic cooking skills, as before leaving for university I became the main cook of my household, and then at university I began experimenting more so I am now quite a good cook. I would walk further to the big shops in the evening to get the reduced food and make the most of the free food →

offered by my college. I downloaded an app for my bus travel and ensured I got any special offers when they were available.

I switched banks to get the railcard reward, as I used trains quite often and this was a very good deal. Having a savings account and daily bank accounts is quite helpful, as you can put your weekly or monthly budget in your daily account and everything else can be "hidden" in a savings account. Then it can help with budgeting and keeping bills paid.

Tldr: Uni is expensive and confusing. Working and studying can be an extra stressor for Autistic working-class individuals and greatly impact their university performance. Financial support is usually only available to those with a diagnosis, and now they can take years. Money management can be stressful, paying rent, bills, food prices skyrocketing and going into an overdraft can seem daunting. Don't be afraid to ask your university for help – there should be financial support available.

Stacey, *Autistic psychology student*

Chapter 5: Staying safe

Keeping yourself safe and happy is the most important thing while you are at university, and staying safe is not as simple as locking the door behind you. You should consider protecting yourself and others from disease and illness, as well as protecting the mental health of yourself and those around you. These are not always fun topics to discuss, and they are often neglected during school PSHE days, but as you head off to university, it is necessary to be equipped with the knowledge and skills to help not only yourself, but also others, from harm.

> **This chapter will talk about sex, drugs, and alcohol, and will refer to sexual violence and spiking.**

Consent

Consent is quite simply *permission* for something to happen. This covers all aspects of your life from your medical care, your personal life choices, and of course your sexual activity. No one should be able to make decisions on your behalf without your consent, and you should never feel like you have to do anything. This goes for drinking, having sex, or going out to a club: everything is your decision.

Consent must be **informed**. This means it cannot be given if you do not have all the information available: for example, you cannot consent to a medical procedure if you are not told of the possible risks and different outcomes of said procedure. You also cannot consent if you do not have the **capacity**: this can mean if you are under the influence of drugs or alcohol. Age also informs capacity, for example, a 12-year-old cannot give consent to sexual activity as they are deemed not to have the capacity. Furthermore, consent must be **freely given**, this means it was your decision, and you were not under any pressure from external sources. This is often associated with 'enthusiastic' consent, where someone is positive and coherent about their decisions. Finally, consent can be **revoked**. Consent is not a blanket decision and cannot occur if it cannot be reversed if necessary. This could mean saying you would like an alcoholic drink, but when it has been poured, deciding you want to stay on the water.

No one can make you drink. The same goes for sexual activity, someone might say they want to have sex, but change their mind during the act – being able to stop, to change your mind, to revoke consent, is imperative.

Consent must be:

■ Informed.

■ Within capacity.

■ Freely given.

■ Reversible.

Case study: Jenny

Jenny and her boyfriend have been going out for a year. He comes to visit her at university and they go out with her friends. Jenny has a lot to drink, and in the morning she wakes up next to her boyfriend and he tells her they had sex last night. She remembers vaguely this happening but knows she was very drunk.

Did Jenny consent?

No. As she was drunk, Jenny did not have the **capacity** to consent to sexual activity. People must not only be fully conscious, but have full ability to give consent and make decisions. Drink and drugs affect a person's ability to make decisions, and therefore they cannot give consent.

Case study: Susie

Susie has just started at university and gets on well with all her flatmates. Susie is transgender, and when she was at school, she went by he/him pronouns. A friend from school comes to visit her and is chatting to her flatmates. The friend tells them that Susie 'used to be a he'. This makes Susie very upset as she had wanted a new start at university, and doesn't feel like anyone needs to know that information about her. Her flatmates ask her later what her 'old name' used to be and she feels like she has to tell them.

Did Susie consent?

No. Susie did not consent to this information about her being shared, this information was hers to disclose and should be **freely given by her**. Always check before disclosing potentially sensitive information about other people, this includes information about gender identity, sexuality and disability.

Case study: Tom

Tom shares his university room with Jack. They get on well, but Jack often goes out clubbing and comes home late. One night Tom is woken up and realises that Jack is having sex with someone in the room. Tom feels very uncomfortable and pretends to be asleep. In the morning, he pretends he didn't know Jack had had someone round.

Did Tom consent?

No. Tom did not give consent to sexual activity happening in his room. Even though he was not physically involved, people need to consent to **seeing** sexual activity. Flashing and having sex in public are illegal because other people are not consenting to view the sexual activity taking place in front of them. Tom did not consent to Jack having sex in his room.

Case study: Harry

Harry is at a party in someone's house and has decided not to drink as he has an early lecture the next morning. He is having a good time and is carrying around a diet coke. When he finishes, his friend Martha brings him a drink in a glass that looks like coke, he thanks her and drinks it. Later he feels slightly dizzy, and he realises that the drink must have had alcohol in it.

Did Harry consent?

No. Harry was not **informed** that the drink contained alcohol. Purposely adding alcohol or drugs to someone's drink without them knowing is known as **spiking** and is **illegal**. If you suspect your drink may have been tampered with, stop drinking it immediately, and seek help from a sober friend or staff member.

Case study: Jay

Jay is on a dating app talking to a fellow student. They are exchanging flirty messages. While they are talking, the student sends Jay a picture of their penis. Jay is shocked and uncomfortable and chooses not to respond, Jay unmatches with them.

Did Jay consent?

No. Jay did not **ask** for this picture. People need to consent to receiving or viewing sexual material. This goes for personal pictures or pornography. Jay can report the other users of the app to the app itself and speak to someone at the university if they want to. 'Cyberflashing' is a crime, and someone can be sentenced and receive a criminal record if they send someone an indecent image without consent.

Case study: Pheobe

Pheobe is in her second year at university and has started seeing someone in her halls. One night, the person suggests they try having anal sex. Pheobe has never done this before but would like to try it. They discuss what they each like and don't like, and that they can stop at any time if either of them wants to, and they agree to use a condom. The next day Pheobe decides that, although she enjoyed herself, she probably doesn't want to do it again, and her partner says he feels the same.

Did Pheobe consent?

Yes. Pheobe discussed her desires beforehand and they both consented to anal sex. They both knew they could stop at any time, so consent was **reversible**.

Sex

The word sex covers so much more than the reproductive health information that schools are required to teach. Sex education specific to people from the LGBTQ+ community is still not universal, which is particularly relevant for Autistic young people who are more likely to belong to this community. In this section I will talk about sex, and staying safe while having sexual contact. Sexual contact can be defined as 'anything from a kiss to intercourse' or, like sexual activity, can include both kissing and intercourse. For some, sexual activity may also extend to photos, videos, phone calls or instant messaging.

Many Autistic people identify as asexual, and therefore you may not feel that this chapter is for you. However, it is still useful to learn the facts so that you can help others in your life, as you never know when the information might come in useful.

Staying safe

Safe sex is not just about preventing pregnancy, it is not even just about wearing a condom. Safe covers all aspects of sexual activity that protect you or someone else from potential negative outcomes. Unfortunately, Autistic people are more at risk of sexual assault, and of being in unsafe or unhealthy relationships, and while these things are *never* a victim's fault, it is important to know what these things look like in order spot the signs for yourself and others.

Condoms

Condoms are the only way to prevent STIs from anal or vaginal sex, and they can also protect against unwanted pregnancy. Condoms should also be worn for oral sex to prevent STIs of the throat and neck. Condoms can go on a penis, sex toys, and fingers, and create a barrier between you and the other person, to prevent viruses and bacteria from passing between you. In vaginal sex, they can also prevent sperm from

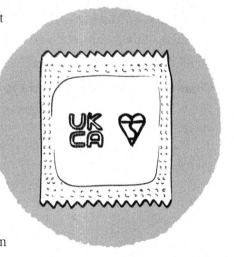

entering the vagina, so that pregnancy does not occur. You can buy condoms from pharmacies, supermarkets, corner shops, or online. When buying online, stick to known brands approved or provided by the NHS such as Durex and Pasante, and avoid novelty condoms as these may not be tested to the same standards. There is a way to check if the condom you have is certified: check on the packet for a BSI kite mark and a UKCA (UK Conformity Assessed) or CE (European Conformity), which mean it is approved. There should also be an expiry date, and you should never use a condom if it is past its expiry.

You can get condoms for free from sexual health clinics and from pharmacies using a C-Card. Some services also post them to you for free – search for 'free condoms in post' along with your town or postcode, to see if there is a service in your area.

Certain places will require you to be under 25 years old, but some, like sexual health clinics, will provide free condoms to all ages.

STIs

Sexually transmitted infections (STIs) are very common, and most are easily treatable, but it is better to avoid getting them in the first place. I could dedicate a whole section to each STI, but I will focus on some of the most common; details about all the STIs out there, and what to look out for can be found on the NHS website. An important message to take away from this section is that **STIs can have no symptoms**. This means you may not know you have one, but it is still damaging your body. Therefore, if you are having any kind of sexual contact, make sure you are getting tested regularly. You can order online tests, which you can do in your own room or bathroom, so you do not necessarily need to attend a clinic or doctor's office unless you have symptoms.

Chlamydia, gonorrhoea and syphilis

These are three of the most common STIs in the UK, with Chlamydia being the most common. They all have various unpleasant symptoms such as unusual discharge from the penis or vagina, pain when urinating, and stomach aches. If you go for an STI test, these three and HIV will be the ones they test for via blood and urine. Left untreated, these can lead to infertility, and they often have no symptoms at all.

HPV

HPV is one of the most common viruses around, and eight out of ten people will have this at some point. There are hundreds of strains, and most cause no symptoms at all, however some can be uncomfortable and lead to genital warts, and a few are dangerous and can lead to cancer. It is not always transmitted through sex, but a good way to prevent catching it is through practising safe sex and always using a condom or dental dam. You should also make sure you have had the HPV vaccination before you start university, as this will help protect against the most dangerous strains of HPV.

If it applies to you, it is also important to go for your smear tests once you get invited. This will be around the age of 24/25. This test looks for HPV on your cervix. Normally the presence of HPV is nothing to worry about, but if it is there, doctors will check your cells for any changes that could lead to cancer, so they can remove them before they get to this stage. For more information about smear tests and cervical changes, Jo's Trust is a great source; the webpage is in the resources section of the book.

HSV

Cold sores are caused by the herpes simplex virus, most commonly picked up in childhood through being kissed by adoring aunts or from sharing a water bottle with a friend. They can flare up at times of stress or illness throughout your life. What we are often not told, probably because we use the sanitised term 'cold sore' rather than herpes when it is on our face, is that this can lead to an STI (sexually transmitted infection) on the genitals of someone else if oral sex is performed. If you touch your mouth and then touch someone's genitals, it can also be passed on this way. Herpes often causes no symptoms, or symptoms that are very mild, but occasionally it can result in painful sores, and serious complications if contracted in certain areas such as around the eyes. This shows the importance of protecting yourself and others during oral and digital (using your hands) sexual contact. If you or someone else has an active cold sore, do not kiss or have oral sex; although the virus can be passed on when no sores are present, it is more likely to be passed on when there are.

HIV

We have come a long way as a society since the human immunodeficiency virus (HIV) was discovered in the 1980s. A person diagnosed quickly after transmission, and who takes the recommended treatment, will have an average life expectancy, and the drugs they take can mean that the HIV is not transmissible through their blood or through sex. Untreated, however, HIV can lead to acquired immune deficiency syndrome (AIDS), which can be fatal. While AIDS cannot be transmitted, HIV can, and the virus is still prevalent due to the many people going untested, highlighting the need for safe sex, and regular STI testing. HIV can be avoided by having safe sex, and through certain preventative measures such as PEP and PrEP.

Post-exposure prophylaxis (PEP/PEPSE) and pre-exposure prophylaxis (PrEP) are drugs which can prevent a person from catching HIV. PEP is taken after you may have been exposed to the HIV virus, either through unprotected sex, needle use, or if a condom splits and you believe the person may be HIV positive. PEP is taken as a one-off and needs to be taken soon after exposure. PrEP is a drug you take regularly, and can prevent you from

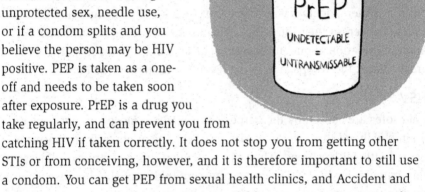

catching HIV if taken correctly. It does not stop you from getting other STIs or from conceiving, however, and it is therefore important to still use a condom. You can get PEP from sexual health clinics, and Accident and Emergency Services, whereas PrEP is available on prescription to people deemed to be at 'high risk' of getting HIV. Look on the NHS and Terrance Higgins Trust websites for more information.

Sexual violence

Sadly, some people commit non-consensual acts against others. This is a very serious offence and is *never* the victim's fault.

If someone touches someone sexually without their consent, this is called sexual assault. This could include, but is not limited to, touching someone's genitals, kissing them, touching their breasts, or penetrating them with a finger or sex toy. When someone penetrates someone with a penis without consent, this is called rape. If someone removes a condom from their penis during sex without the other person knowing or consenting to this, this is also called rape. Rape is a form of sexual assault.

Sexual harassment is a form of sexual violence and can include sexual contact that doesn't involve unwanted touching. This can include, but is not limited to, *unwanted*:

- Sexual comments or noises, e.g. catcalling or wolf-whistling.
- Flirting or sexual advances.
- Sending texts or emails of a sexual nature.
- Discussing sex and people's sex lives.
- Commenting on someone's appearance in a sexual way.
- Taking photos of someone under their clothing.
- Showing someone photos of a sexual nature.

It is the person *receiving* the behaviour who decides if it was unwanted or not, not the person *doing* the behaviour.

Indecent exposure is another form of sexual violence, and this includes 'flashing', where someone exposes their genitals to someone, often in public, and 'cyber flashing', where someone sends a sexual or nude image or video of themselves to someone without consent, often called a 'dick pic' if it is from someone with a penis.

Some victims of sexual violence do not like to be called 'victims', and instead use the term 'survivor'. It is up to the person to decide themselves what term they would like to use.

If you or someone you know has been raped or sexually assaulted, one of the first steps is to consider attending a sexual assault referral centre (SARC). It can be difficult to take this step, as often people want to stay home and forget it ever happened, however, if they ever do want to report it to the police, a SARC can take forensic information that is only available soon after the assault. They will ask you to try not to go to the loo, shower, or change clothes before attending the centre, this is so they can get as much evidence as possible. At the centres, there are also specialist counsellors and people who can give you support and advice. Details of where to find your nearest SARC are at the back of the book.

It is common for people to blame themselves for experiencing sexual violence. However, it is important to know that it is never the victim's fault, and nothing someone says, or wears, makes it any more their fault or any less worthy of support. In America, and some other countries, it is common for people to carry self-defence items such as pepper spray or a 'mace', these are **illegal in the UK**, and you could be arrested for carrying a weapon.

Hopefully, you never need to use this information, but you can use it to support and inform others.

Alcohol

Alcohol consumption at university has been going down over the years. Back when students would get large grants from the government, and therefore have disposable income, there was a large drinking culture at UK universities. However, either because students these days are more strapped for cash, or because young people today tend to drink less than their predecessors, there is less alcohol consumption occurring across institutions. In fact, around one in six students do not drink at all. This is not to say alcohol is no longer an issue, and university is often the first place many people have their first drink (and second, and tenth), but the drinking culture will most likely not be as bad as your parents or grandparents remember it being, which is a good thing for everyone!

Alcohol changes your mood and the ways in which you think and behave. It is a 'depressant', and so it makes you tired and lethargic (although you may feel more energetic in the short term), it can also cause low mood and anxiety, including social anxiety, in many. Some Autistic people do not like the effects alcohol has on them, saying they worry they cannot mask as well around non-Autistic people when they have had a drink, and this makes them anxious. However, some Autistic people report finding that alcohol makes them feel more relaxed around others, and allows them to be more sociable, without the pressures of masking they usually face. Every person will experience alcohol differently, and as long as you are safe and being responsible and healthy, many people can enjoy drinking at university.

I am a summer-born baby, so I was one of the many students who discovered alcohol during my freshers' week at university, as I had only just turned 18. I had always thought of alcohol as being a bit gross; wine and beer had left a bitter taste in my mouth. However, that was before I arrived at university and discovered the 'alcopop'! Suddenly, there were sugary drinks that tasted like juice, and it was too easy to forget they were alcoholic. Hence followed a week of me learning the effects the hard way!

This is the important thing to remember, *there is no safe level of alcohol consumption.* There used to be recommended weekly amounts which were considered 'safe' and healthy; however, these have been removed, and those drinking less than 14 units a week are considered 'low-risk', but this is not the same as no-risk.

SINGLE SPIRIT SHOT (25ml)
1 UNIT

GLASS OF WINE (125ml)
2.2 UNITS

CAN OF BEER (440ml)
2.4 UNITS

PINT OF BEER (low - high strength)
2-3 UNITS

COCKTAIL (3 x 25 ml spirit measures)
3 UNITS

A unit of alcohol is roughly the amount your body can process in an hour, this means that, in theory, if you had a shot of 40% alcohol (e.g., vodka), it would be out of your system within an hour. A glass of wine would take two or three hours. This is for an average adult, however, and some people process alcohol more slowly than others. Therefore, if driving or operating machinery, the best advice is to have no alcohol at all in the hours leading up to it, to ensure your alcohol levels are zero. Another important thing to remember is that there is no way to get alcohol out of your system: a strong coffee, a fried breakfast, a cold shower, vomiting: none of these will lower your blood alcohol levels, only time can sober someone up. If you have had a lot of alcohol the night before, you may not be safe to drive the next morning, even though you may feel rested and sober after sleeping.

Drugs

Something I found fascinating at school was when they would bring in the 'drugs van', which contained examples of the most common illegal substances (behind several layers of reinforced glass) so we could see what they actually looked like. Much like with sex and alcohol, I do not believe that ignorance will lead to less drug taking. I think the more you know, the better informed you are to make the right decisions for your health and well-being.

I thought that when I started university, I would be inundated with offers of drugs: a plethora of opportunities to try out my well-practised 'just say no' approach we had learned in PSHE lessons. But it was not like that. I was offered drugs in a club maybe once during my entire undergraduate degree, and although I knew of people or friends who did drugs, these were never offered to me at parties or when hanging out. Statistics show that the usage of drugs is decreasing with every generation, so you may not get offered drugs the whole time you are at university. Or you may indeed be regularly in contact with people taking, and offering, drugs. You might not get offered drugs at university but may find yourself being asked if you want to chip in at an after-work party in your 20s. What is important is to know the facts, and for this I would recommend the website Frank (talktofrank.com). This website tells you what drugs look taste and smell like, why people take them, and the risks associated with them. If you hear a term you do not know, you can search it on the site too, to see if it is slang for a drug.

> **Website:** www.talktofrank.com for no-nonsense facts about drugs, the law, and their effects.

> **Drugs testing:** this is offered in some parts of the country and at some festivals. It is where someone will take the drug you have been given (pill, power etc.) and test it to see if it really is what you were told it is. It is then up to you if you take it. This is a safer way to do drugs but does not eliminate risk.

At the end of the day, it is your decision whether or not to take drugs. I could talk about the law, life sentences, and criminal records, or health, people dying at festivals, or ending up with life-limiting injuries. But you know this. My telling you not to take drugs while at university does not mean that's what you'll do. But I will say this: personally, as an Autistic person, unpredictability is something I really struggle with, and this is particularly true when it comes to drugs. You do not know how you will react. You also do not know what is in the drugs you are taking if they haven't been tested or approved. You could be swallowing a pill of ecstasy, or of cyanide for all you know, and powders such as cocaine are often cut with all sorts of nasty pharmaceuticals and by-products. You could even have an allergic reaction to the ingredients. To me, this is too many variables, and the unpredictability of illegal drugs is probably the most dangerous thing about them.

Spiking

Sadly, bars and clubs are places where spiking can take place. Cases of spiking have risen dramatically in recent years, along with perpetrators using new ways of spiking people, such as through needles. Spiking is very serious, and if you think you have been attacked, head to your nearest A&E department straight away. It is never the victim's fault if they have been spiked.

> **Spiking:** Adding alcohol or a drug to someone's drink, food or body without them realising.

There are a number of ways you can try and protect yourself:

- Never leave your drink unattended.
- Always take your drink from the bartender, not from anyone else. If someone wants to buy you a drink, go with them to the bar.
- Hold your friends' drinks for them when they go to the loo.
- Use your thumb to cover the top of a bottle when you are not drinking from it.

■ Use a drink cover or anti-spiking cap to prevent anything from being added to your drink.

Unfortunately, there aren't as many ways to prevent needle spiking, so look out for signs you are unwell such as dizziness, sleepiness or sweating. Get yourself to safety as soon as possible, and then go to your nearest hospital.

If you are ever scared, feel unsafe, or just want to leave and don't know how, most bars and clubs have a policy called 'Ask for Angela', where you can approach any member of staff and ask if you can talk to Angela. They will help you get out and call you a taxi or ambulance if needed.

Illness

We have a responsibility to others to make sure we are not passing on nasty bugs and viruses, and we can do this through simple things such as covering our mouths when we cough or wearing a mask if we are unwell. Make sure you have all the vaccinations you need, and stay up to date with flu jabs each year (provided through some universities, or available at pharmacies). Many people can't have these vaccines, so by you having them, you will reduce the spread of infection, as well as protect yourself from becoming ill. Taking time off from your studies because you are unwell is bad, but worse when it could have been avoided!

If you are ill, take time to get better, rest, and look after yourself. Pushing yourself too much, or too soon will make you feel worse in the long run, and will delay you getting better. Reach out to lecturers if you are off sick, and contact your GP or other NHS services for help if you are worried about your health, or you have an illness that has gone on longer than a week and is stopping you from doing the things you would normally do. Keep an eye on yourself and others around you. Specifically, look out for symptoms of common dangerous illnesses such as meningitis and sepsis (see p.178), as these are often missed.

Chapter 6: Finding your people

Once you have settled into university and have survived your first week or two, it is time to think about how to make the most out of your university experience: how to find friends and thrive. This is an incredible time of your life, with endless opportunities and adventures to be had, and wonderful, interesting people to meet and learn about. That's before you get to the content of your course, which can be fascinating, challenging and rewarding, as you learn more and more about your passions and interests. However, this is not always a smooth road, and this section will help you to learn how to make the most of being at university.

'Universities are huge places compared to schools and colleges, with even the small ones having a couple of thousand students, while the biggest can have tens of thousands of students. In here are people you will gel with, and become friends with, maybe even spend the rest of your life with, but also people you will disagree with on almost every word they say and wish to be as far away from as possible! Joining clubs and societies is a good way to find people who have similar interests, →

and many universities have disabled students' associations, or Autistic student groups, where you can find other people with similar experiences and needs. Research has shown that Autistic people often enjoy the company of other Autistic people, so these groups can be great places to make new friends and to give and receive peer support.

'University can feel vast and overwhelming. However, the large number of students means that the student community is diverse. There are a multitude of clubs, societies and groups for every niche interest and hobby. Fresher's week is a great time to try out these societies and to see what is on offer. Societies are often groups of like-minded people, with a common interest, and so are a fantastic way to meet people. I would recommend committing yourself to one or two societies, in order to fully immerse yourself in the community it creates. Although there can be pressure to mask heavily when arriving at university, I would advise trying to be your authentic self from the start, even if you feel that you do not "fit in" with your flatmates – you are much more likely to meet like-minded people that way. Lectures and tutorials are also a great way to get to know peers on your course; I found seminars and tutorials easier to strike up conversations with people, as they are generally smaller and more intimate groups. University is big – do not worry if you do not find "your people" straight away; it is rare for people to meet lifelong friends at the start of term, for many it takes months or even years.

Sophie Taylor-Davies, *Autistic English literature student*

As Sophie says, do not expect to find your best friends forever, or a life partner, during your first year at university. Not all relationships, be they romantic or friendships, last forever, and what is important is that you enjoy them while they last, and end them when they no longer work or bring you joy. When you start university, you may find that there are large groups of friends; this is common when people live in flats, as they will naturally group together, and then grow with additional people as time goes on. Like many Autistic people, I always found friendships easier one-on-one, and societies and associations are good places to diverge from these large groups.

Autistic people often develop more intense friendships and relationships than non-Autistic people, and this comes with its own benefits and challenges. When you first start university, you may be overwhelmed by the number of amazing people you meet and how much you have in common. This can lead to strong bonds forming very quickly, as you both explore each other's similar interests. This can be incredibly rewarding, but it is important to remember to 'keep your options open', as people say, so that you do not cut yourself off from other potential friendships. Spending all your time with one or two people can feel very safe and secure, but it can stop you from meeting other people to also be friends with. Meeting and spending time with a variety of people means that if for any reason you no longer want to be friends with one of those people, you still have others to hang around with and do activities with.

Coming out

I always found it much easier to tell people that I was queer than to tell them I was Autistic. For me, there was more stigma around Autism than there was concerning my sexuality. I knew what to expect when I told people I had a girlfriend, and it was positive 99% of the time. When I came out as Autistic, it could be positive, or it could be 'I'm so sorry' or 'Will your kids have it too?' The best response I have found to disclosing my Autistic status is the 'Oh, me too!', and you may find that you have helped someone else to come out where before they were too nervous to disclose.

I think things are getting better every year, so I really hope you won't have any negative experiences of coming out as Autistic, but it is still your decision if and when you disclose your Autistic status. You deserve to own your narrative, and therefore you can choose who knows what about you. It is also not your job to educate people; you can explain things to them if you want to, or you can direct them towards resources such as the National Autistic Society, but you have no obligation to do either.

109

Going 'out out'

I thought I would hate nightclubs: they are loud, crowded and hot – three things I hate. However, it turned out that I loved them; it was a chance to let my hair down, sing, dance, and interact without the worries of the nuances of social interactions. I couldn't say anything wrong if nobody could hear me! However, this may not be the case for you, and that's okay – nightclubs are not a compulsory part of university. But if you do go 'out out', you might want to be prepared in advance for what to expect.

Firstly, you may experience a lot of peer pressure to go out – some see it as a rite of passage into university life, which is absolutely not true. However, there will be many people, away from home for the first time, who are excited to explore things they did not have the freedom to explore at home, such as going to nightclubs. These people might not understand why someone else does not want to join them, and therefore try and pressure others into joining them. Finding alternative activities you enjoy is important if you do not want to go clubbing, to avoid feeling left out. There will be many people who do not like clubbing, it is just a case of finding them. Looking at the students' union website for clubs and societies that meet in the evenings, and attending a few introductory sessions of these can help you to build up a picture of what you enjoy doing, and who you enjoy doing it with.

'University is notorious for a culture of nights out, partying and clubbing. This brings certain pressures, expectations and anxieties that Autistic students are particularly vulnerable to. Nights out can be tricky for us – changes in routines and precarious plans, sensory overloads and unprecedented social exposure. However, there are ways around this. Firstly, there is absolutely no reason to force yourself to go on nights out if it is not an experience you enjoy. If it is, but there are aspects that pose challenges, there are ways to make the night out adaptable – whether it be location, choice of people, outfit, time etc. Secondly, a 'night out' does not solely equate to clubbing. Personally, I forced myself out clubbing a handful of times before finally admitting to myself that it just wasn't for me. However, this does not mean that I miss out socially. I regularly go on pub trips with friends and attend parties or small social gatherings. The difference for me is who I am with. I have close friends who I feel less pressure to mask around and who I am able to be honest with when I need to leave.

One aspect of university culture to use is 'pres' (pre-drinks). These are generally hosted at a person's flat or a cheap pub. Pres are often the most social part of a night out, and I find them to be the least anxiety-provoking; a smaller group in a familiar setting. I regularly just attend the pre-drinks and skip the clubbing part altogether. This means I still feel included and have socialised in a safe environment without putting myself through the distress and exhaustion of a club. It is also worth researching your area, as accessible clubbing spaces do exist, although rare. One example of this is Spectrum, a club night run by and catered to the queer neurodivergent community in London.

Sophie Taylor-Davies, *Autistic English literature student*

As Sophie describes, whether you enjoy a quiet night in, a few pre-drinks, or full-on clubbing, there are many options available. It is important to consider the sensory issues around nightclubs and bars. Clubs are very loud, and this can be a lot for Autistic people. Earbuds like Loop can really help with this; you can still hear what is going on, but the noise is dampened somewhat. This can delay sensory overload and allow you to enjoy your night for longer. Be aware of your body and how you are feeling and listen to it when it tells you you've had enough.

Some universities offer city trips, where you can experience nightclubs and bars in a different town or city. I went on one of these but did not like the fact that I had to wait for the bus home. If, like me, you like to always have an exit option, consider a back-up plan before you go on one of these trips, to ensure you are not stuck somewhere if you decide you want to go home early.

Junior common rooms (JCRs)

Some universities, especially collegiate universities, will have **JCRs**. These are physical spaces for students in the same college or halls, often with their own bar, but it also refers to the group of students themselves. They can be run by students, often elected by members of the JCR, or by the hall's coordinators, and are one of the many communities you will have at university. A lot of the events and activities in your first few weeks of term will be organised by your JCR if you have one. The good thing about JCR-run events is that you will have a common living space with others, meaning you don't have to traipse across campus to attend a pub quiz or craft evening. However, you might find you have more in common in communities based on similar interests, such as societies or clubs run within the JCR or the Students' Union.

Students' union

The **students' union** is a student organisation dedicated to social activities, student representation, and support of the students at its university. It usually has its own building, and its purpose is to promote the interests of students. They have different names across the UK, and can also be known as student associations, or guilds. Most UK students' unions are affiliated with the National Union of Students (NUS).

A certain amount of politics usually surrounds students' unions, and student politics in general is a fraught area. Many students use students' unions to launch their own political or journalistic careers, so the environment can sometimes be complex. Don't let this stop you from getting involved, however, as it is there for you, and to support you and all students in their student journeys. They also organise events, societies and opportunities for all students, which are always worth getting involved in.

A students' union offers a variety of services, from checking over rental contracts to lobbying on behalf of students, and they can often be the first point of call for support in any disputes between students and the university. You are automatically a member of the students' union when you start at university, and this allows you to access many discounts and offers from retailers with your NUS card or similar.

Societies

The number and variety of societies available at universities is by far one of the greatest parts of university life. They offer great social opportunities within structured environments, which can be perfect for Autistic people. There are different types of society, roughly divided into: minority representation, academic, political, religious, and common interest. Nearly all universities will have societies or groups for minority groups such as LGBTQ+, disabled, women, mature students, and black people. Not all universities will have all of these, but there is always the option to start your own! In terms of academic societies, these are often for the larger cohorts, such as law students, but will exist for smaller subjects too. They are a chance to get together with fellow students studying your degree, or with an interest in your area, and discuss topics, or listen to speakers. Political societies, including debating societies, can be fun, if fraught with student politics. There are often societies for the major political parties, and many of these students go on to have careers in politics. There will also be campaign groups for certain issues, who may hold protests or boycotts across the university year.

Religious societies usually welcome people of all faiths and can be a good place to meet friendly faces (and often to get free pizza!). There are usually societies for the major religions, and occasionally those for smaller organised groups, be they religious or spiritual. For common interests, film societies are common, as are those around certain games like chess or E-sports. Then there are the more 'out there' societies, some of my favourites are:

- Hummus Society (multiple universities).
- Nicolas Cage Appreciation Society (University of Sussex).
- Kettle Society (University of Nottingham).
- Zombie Apocalypse Survival Society (University of Manchester).
- Robot Football Society (University of Plymouth).

Many universities now have Autistic or neurodivergent societies, which I would encourage you to try at least once. Autistic people are known to often get on well with other Autistic people, and this is the perfect place

to meet them. When I went to the Autistic society at my university, we played Cards Against Muggles, and there was a box of fidget toys for people to play with – I felt very welcome! Societies are also a good way to test out your organisational and leadership skills; a society you join in the first year might be looking for a president or someone to manage the finances. These roles are often elected, so you can try your hand at student democracy while you're at it!

At the freshers' fair, there are usually stalls for each society, where you can talk to current members and sign up to their mailing lists or join their social media page. They often also have bribe treats at these stalls to encourage you to join. My advice is to sign up for everything you think looks interesting! Chances are you won't ever go to half of them, but it gives you options, and you never know, robot football could be your new passion.

Sports

You will notice on your timetable that you likely have nothing on a Wednesday afternoon, this is because, at most UK universities, this time is dedicated to sports. There is always the chance to get involved in sport at university, even if, like me, you are not the most athletic. There are elite teams which will compete against other universities and will train regularly, often funded by the university. However, there are also smaller teams, like the women's football team I joined; we only had seven players, but we turned up and got beaten every week, and it was a great way to get out and do some exercise! There are even novelty sports like Quidditch and Ultimate Frisbee, if traditional sports don't appeal to you.

Most sports teams will organise 'socials' where the team members get together and go to bars or clubs. These often happen on Wednesday nights, or after training. Sometimes this will involve costumes or silly games, which should be optional. Unfortunately, there is a culture at some universities, and some sports teams, of **'initiations'** or **'hazing'**, which is where someone is expected to take part in a humiliating or dangerous activity in order to gain access to the group.

> **Hazing:** An activity which is humiliating or dangerous, which someone is expected to take part in in order to gain group membership.

Hazings and initiations are not allowed at universities, but unfortunately they do still happen. These often involve expecting people to drink dangerous levels of alcohol, or take part in stunts which are illegal and/or dangerous, and are much more common in men's teams and societies, especially those for football and rugby. Initiations and hazings can be extremely dangerous, and people have died taking part in them, so now more than ever is a time not to succumb to peer pressure. No society or sports team should deny you membership because you do not wish to partake in a hazing. If you feel able to, report this behaviour to the university to prevent it from continuing. Sports and societies should be fun and enjoyable; if they stop being so, remove yourself from the situation, or report those making you feel uncomfortable.

Chapter 7: Staying on track academically

University is a step up in every way when it comes to academia and what is expected of you, and this can be a shock to many Autistic people. The new challenge can be exciting, but also daunting compared to the small classes and high levels of support at school or college. This chapter will look at some helpful strategies, as well as discuss key academic terms you need to know before starting your degree, such as plagiarism and referencing. It will then discuss different academic opportunities you may have and how to make the most out of your degree.

Strategies

My advice would be to nail these strategies in your first year, right from the outset, as your second and third years will be much more challenging academically, so you will be prepared. With all of these strategies, try and stay flexible. Many people say flexibility doesn't come naturally to Autistic people, but I would disagree – when we are the ones in charge of the flexibility we can be excellent at it. If you find that a certain way of studying isn't working for you, don't be afraid to change it so that your time is spent most effectively.

Create a timetable

For many, especially those in the arts and humanities, your timetable will look a lot emptier than when you were at school, but don't be fooled into thinking you have free time outside of this! For each hour in lectures, you are usually expected to do at least one hour of reading or homework. Immediately, or as soon after each lecture or seminar as possible, make some time to go over what has been covered, consolidate

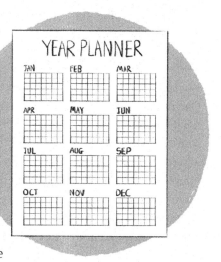

your notes, and complete any tasks that have arisen. In your 'free' hours, allocate some time to each module for extra studying, or working on assignments for that topic. Investing in a wall planner, or making your own, can be very useful. I have a full-year one, which may be massive, but it shows me every month of the year in one go, which helps me to visualise the time between events. Cross off each day once it's passed, and put key deadlines or exams in a different colour.

Be prepared

Much like the Scout motto suggests, it is important to be ready for your lectures and seminars. This includes doing any compulsory reading in advance and checking to see what topic will be covered. This will help not only you but also any less-organised friends who will no doubt message in the group chat asking, 'Was there any homework?', 20 minutes before the seminar. If you are doing a practical subject, make sure you have everything you need, such as a lab coat or goggles, as you may not be allowed to take part in the activity if you do not have the correct equipment.

Make clear notes

You will thank yourself when it comes to exam season! Decide early on how you will make notes: will you use a tablet or laptop, or will you write them down? How will you store them? I hand-wrote mine and then stored the pages in individual folders for each module, but many people prefer to work online. Make sure you label your notes correctly, so when you are looking for a certain week, or a particular topic, you know where to go looking. During my lectures, if there was a word I didn't understand or a reference I wanted to look up, I would put a star next to it. After each lecture, I would go back to all my starred items and highlight them once I had looked them up.

Talk to other students

Having a regular time to meet with others on your course is invaluable. One of the hardest parts of being a student during the pandemic was not having other students to discuss my degree with. As an Autistic person, sometimes the last thing you want to do after an intense seminar is to talk to other people, and that's okay. But if there are study groups, or you know other people on your course that you get on with, sitting down to discuss the lecture or to debate a topic that was covered is very valuable. During my master's degree, we would all head across the road to Starbucks and complain about how difficult one of our modules was (and have a moan about how it was covered – I didn't say you had to discuss positive things!) But doing this helped us to destress and decompress, as well as to consolidate what we had learned, even if it sometimes wasn't very much! It can also be useful to know people in the years above you taking the same degree, as they can help you to understand certain topics and will be a good source of information on what to expect in the years to come, and which modules they would recommend. Societies aimed at particular areas of study, such as the History Society, for example, can be a good place to meet students in the year above. Some universities will even arrange buddying schemes where you are paired with someone on the same course as you but in a different year. Take advantage of this if it is available to you.

Make use of staff office hours

Most staff will have a time each week when their door is open for students to come and ask questions. Lots of students never use this, and it is a shame because your lecturers are the most knowledgeable people about your course and subject. If there is something you don't understand, or you are unsure if you are approaching an assignment the correct way, pop in during these hours to ask for help – it's what they're there for!

Check your emails

You might not be used to checking your emails every day, but when you're at university it becomes a necessity. Lectures could be cancelled on the day, or new material sent out in advance of a seminar. There are opportunities, extra talks from visiting academics, and society updates all sent out via email, and you don't want to miss out on these. Your university may also have an online system you need to check, although this differs by institution, and many will send out an email to let you know when things like a new grade or assignment feedback has been uploaded.

Create a good working environment

Find when and where you work best; for some, this will be at 1am in your room as an idea strikes you just as you're about to go to bed, whereas for others it will be on sunny afternoons in the library café. Minimise distractions that you know don't help you to work: if you like music while you work, great, but if you are doing karaoke to Taylor Swift's latest album, not much of your essay will get written. Maintain a clear workspace wherever you are working – a mess will not help you to concentrate, and you will need space to spread out your notes.

Keep on top of things

It can be easy to let things pile up: first, you miss one lecture, then you forget to watch the recording, then you miss the seminar because you didn't read the paper required for it. Break the cycle before it starts and make sure you keep up to date with your modules. If you find yourself falling behind, don't be afraid to approach your lecturer to ask for an extension on an assignment, or to explain why you haven't done the reading. It is always better to turn up, even if you have missed the previous lecture, and, otherwise, you will just continue to fall behind and it will become unmanageable. Use your holidays to rest and recover, as well as to catch up on any missed work or topics you didn't fully understand.

Stay healthy

You might have once written a great essay while sleep deprived and full of caffeine, but it is not a good strategy in the long term. Make sure you eat well, sleep enough, and stay hydrated. Autistic people often struggle to listen to their bodies or know what their bodies need; if this is the case for you, keep track of when you eat and drink, and set reminders on your phone like 'drink a glass of water', 'have a snack', or 'go to bed'.

Take breaks and have fun

My Vice-Chancellor once told us, 'Don't let your degree get in the way of your education', and this take on the Mark Twain quote is very true. You might be at university to get a degree, but that's not the only reason. Take lots of breaks to decompress, go for walks and meet up with friends. Join societies and sports teams and cook good food. Believe it or not, these things will help with your studying in the long run too.

'There is a wealth of support available to you so take advantage of it! Some key strategies for staying on track are:

- Reach out to your lecturers early, discuss any concerns and let them know how you like to receive feedback. One fantastic lecturer I had knew I wanted a First and marked accordingly. Their support was invaluable in improving my grade.

- Mark out deadlines in a calendar format that suits your working style; wallchart, phone, email-based, whatever will prompt you in good time. Remind yourself of these deadlines often, they creep up quickly!

- Block out dedicated study time on this calendar, stick to it as closely as possible. But leave a contingency – life happens!

- When you study, colour coding tasks according to priority (red, yellow, green is popular) focuses time most efficiently. Use Post-its, to-do lists, or digital resources (e.g. https://goblin.tools) to help you do this.

- Break these tasks down into tiny, accessible steps and create small wins to push you onwards.

- Use both intrinsic and extrinsic motivation. Visualise why you want the degree. What will it help you do? Imagine how good it will feel to achieve it. Spend a couple of minutes pre-study time reframing your mindset – study is an investment in your future. Finish with a reward; chocolate, gaming, TV – whatever works for you.

- Finally, if you are struggling and think you may need an adjustment or extension, contact your university as soon as possible. They will need time to put this in place. Good luck!'

Tracy Smith, *Autistic staff member: university-based Specialist Autism Mentor, funded through the Disabled Students Allowance (see your Disability Services team), who helps students stay focused on their studies and ensure they are working at their best throughout their time at university.*

Deadlines

The feeling of finally submitting an assignment is a great relief, as all that stress is released. However, if you do not submit an assignment on time, your mark will likely be capped at 40%, or be given 0%. Make a list of all your deadlines for every assignment and prioritise them roughly in this order (depending on how much effort each one will take). If you need more time to

complete anything, ask your course leader; they want you to pass as much as you do, so they can usually help you out with some extra days or even a week or two if there's a reason.

> **Extension:** When you are given extra time to work on an assignment past a deadline. This can be due to ill-health, personal circumstances, or other reasons.

Group projects

Many degrees require active participation as part of the ongoing work and assessment in modules. This participation can take the form of presentations and group projects. Group work can be especially challenging for Autistic people, and with the added pressure of the assessment counting towards your grades, this can become an overwhelming task. This is where it is important to talk to your lecturers in advance, to see what reasonable adjustments can be made for you if needed. These can involve: giving the presentation to a smaller group, or even just the lecturer, or being judged on your own contribution to the project rather than the overall result. Here, Luce talks about their experience of group work while an undergraduate:

'I think the Autistics gets the short end of the stick because of inherent integrity and a sense of personal responsibility, the hyper attention to detail, and what can be termed "rigidity". These are traits which are excellent strengths when utilised well and could be an asset – but when coupled with the social dynamics of new people, it can be difficult.

Group work has been the most stymieing part of being in college now because I have been in the workplace and doing large projects in teams for decades, quite successfully. I highly recommend using project management tools and framing it as a learning experience that is valuable for everyone. The methods I've found useful are using a Discord or a spreadsheet with all relevant guidelines, deadlines, details, literature, a central depository of resources and metalinks, clear allocation of responsibilities and having comments on questions that are only resolved when the whole group decides. This also helps document individual effort that has gone into the project, which unfortunately may be necessary. →

Even if you are familiar with collaborative working, navigating projects with other students is a different dynamic. It's been upsetting emotionally for me to mask and blend socially while my grade and future are on the line. I have been frustrated most by group members who don't keep deadlines and who do not hold themselves accountable for their portion of the work. For example, a group member asked me "Do you really think [the teacher] will read the literature we cite to see if it's appropriate?". ARGHHGGH! Often, I don't think about the requirements for the projects the same way, I see the macro or micro relevance and also take into account the lectures and materials comprehensively. I feel others are far too casual about following guidelines. Also, they don't focus or work at the same rate as me and I am left waiting. A quixotic part is either I am picky over details that to others do not matter (e.g., colours used for graphs so that they are accessible) OR I focus on the end result of the project rather than picky details that I feel aren't necessary (e.g., "pretty PowerPoints" for a science presentation). These are things I've been learning to manage.

I think being aware of your personality, and being charitable to yourself, and also to try to be flexible when it comes to others' personalities, are the key. When you start feeling overwhelmed ¬– take a break and try to observe what's happening so that you can either draw a boundary for yourself or to let it go.'

Luce, *Autistic applied linguistics student*

123

Exams and coursework

Many UK universities use the terms 'formative' and 'summative' to describe the types of assessment, and this can be confusing. I always tried to remember 'former' as in 'before' and 'summary' to mean 'at the end'. If in doubt, ask your lecturer whether this assignment counts towards your final grade. There are many different ways of assessing throughout universities, and different disciplines will have different ways of approaching this. The most common methods of assessment are assignments with essay components or problems to solve and exams. However, students can also be asked to provide portfolios, perform music, or present in front of peers and/or staff. For all of these, you will be able to ask for reasonable adjustments, such as presenting in front of fewer people or having longer to complete the task.

> **Formative assessment:** Used to monitor learning and progress, it does not count towards a student's final grade, but can help then to see where they are at academically.

> **Summative assessment:** Used to evaluate student learning formally, with grades counting towards the student's degree or final grade for the year.

Your assignments will have word limits, which you must stick to, otherwise you can lose marks, or the person marking it may just stop reading after the point at which you go over. Some universities allow you to go 10% over or under the word limit, others are more strict and will not mark a word over. Check the policy, but ultimately try and keep to the limits given as closely as possible. Planning out your assignment in advance can help you stick to this. For example, if your essay is 2,000 words, set aside around 250 each for the introduction and conclusion, and keep track of how many words you are using as you write.

Marking

University work is marked differently to how your school work will have been done. Percentages are still used, but these then refer to **degree classifications**. Every piece of work that counts towards your final grade will be marked against these classifications, and the average at the end will decide what kind of degree you are awarded.

> **Degree classification:** The grading levels used to describe attainment at degree level. For undergraduates this goes from a First-class degree to an ordinary degree.

You need 40% to 'pass' at the undergraduate level, and if you do not reach this, you will most likely need to retake that module, or the entire year of work, to move onto the next year of study. Your final degree will most likely be called an 'Honours degree', of which there are four kinds:

- Above 70% is called a 1st, a first-class degree.

- Between 60 and 69% is a 2:1, which stands for an upper second-class degree.

- Between 50 and 59% is a 2:2, a lower second-class degree.

- Between 40 and 49% is a 3rd, a third-class degree.

If you receive at least 40% in all years but your last year, you may be awarded what is called an 'ordinary degree', which is a degree without Honours. Many jobs will only accept degrees if they are Honours degrees. Note that, in Scotland, some classifications are different, so check with your particular institution.

There is a common phrase that 'first year doesn't count', as often (but not always!) the marks from your first year of undergraduate study do not count towards your final degree classification. However, I strongly disagree with this phrase, as firstly you still need to pass in order to progress into your second year of study and secondly, if you wish to do a year abroad or placement, they may look at all your grades to decide, and this will include your first-year grades. Not only that but you'll need the information learned in your first year for the rest of your course, so you need to try hard and learn as much as possible in order to do well in subsequent years.

Referencing

For many, the first time you have to reference your work is at university, and this can take some getting used to. Each department will have its own preferred referencing system, some popular ones include APA (American Psychological Association), Harvard, or Vancouver styles, named after where they originated.

There are two types of citation: 'in-text' refers to those within and at the end of sentences throughout the text, and 'bibliography' or 'reference list' references, which are a list of all references you have used, with the full details, at the end of the piece of work. This list tends to either be organised alphabetically by authors' surnames, or chronologically, by the order they are referred to in the text (numerical systems). There are lots of rules for each system, for example, for papers with more than one author, some will ask you to name the first two authors, followed by 'et al', others will say to name the first three, followed by 'et al', and some will ask you to just give the first author and 'et al', which just means 'and others', who you would then reference in full in the list at the end of the paper.

> **Referencing:** Providing a piece of work with a citation or mention of the source where the information or argument originated.

Each referencing system will have a website and/or book detailing how to reference in their style, which is worth browsing to get to grips with. However, consider also using referencing software, especially if you are using a numerical system such as Vancouver. For my undergraduate degree, I did my references by hand, typing them out exactly, which involves a lot of ensuring the full stops or brackets are in the right place, and that the initial of the person was either before or after their surname (it can change depending on whether they are author or editor). This took up a lot of my time but did help me to get my head around the referencing system's rules.

However, for my PhD, I switched to EndNote, and it was the best decision I made. You can get an add-on for Word or similar, where you can insert the reference in the correct format into your work. This is perfect for saving time, as well as for being able to keep and organise all your references in one place. There are several types of software out there, and some are free, so shop around to find the one that works for you. They are especially useful if you are split across departments which use different referencing styles, as you can insert citations in a particular style depending on which is needed.

Plagiarism

I almost got in trouble for plagiarism during my undergraduate degree. I had completed my essay and handed it in when my friend asked to see my reference list. I sent it across, thinking I was just being helpful, and it was only the references, right? Unbeknownst to me, she copy-and-pasted it to the end of her own essay, which was promptly picked up by the plagiarism software as being identical to my own. This software (the one often used in the UK is called Turnitin) is used by all universities to check electronic submissions, it checks for similarities between your manuscript and other essays across the whole country (and sometimes the world!), as well as published papers and books. This was an example of collusion, and luckily it was not an official assignment, a 'summative', but was a practice one, a 'formative'. But it taught me an important lesson about plagiarism and what counts as breaking the rules.

> **Plagiarism:** Including any idea or any language from someone else in your work without giving due credit by citing and referencing the source.

> **Collusion:** When students work together to complete an assessment that should have been completed independently.

This example of plagiarism was a mistake and thankfully had no repercussions other than reminding me what the rules were. However, some forms of plagiarism are more obvious and can have serious consequences, including being removed from the university or having your degree taken off you if you have already graduated. **Always cite your sources**, and never copy and paste into your work.

Contract cheating is another form of plagiarism, and is sadly quite common in universities; services exist now where you can pay for someone else to write an essay for you, or they will complete mathematics questions. Not only are these expensive and against the rules, but they often also produce incorrect answers or low grades. Furthermore, they will often share these answers online for others to buy, so your work will be identical to many others who are also using the service.

The bottom line is that the repercussions of cheating are always worse than a low grade, or going to your lecturer and admitting that you are struggling. They do not want you to fail, or to drop out, and will try and help you to get to the level you need to be. Don't waste your money and your degree.

> **Contract cheating:** When someone else completes an assessment for you. It is often in exchange for some form of payment, but not always.

Dealing with uncertainty in academia

When completing your A-Levels, there will generally have been a 'right answer' for the majority of situations. In my physics classes, we learned equations, figures and distances off by heart; in geography we learned the magnitude of an earthquake or the impact of the 1987 storm on the UK. Even if there was ambiguity, such as in English literature, there were agreed-upon ways of addressing problems. You might disagree with your English teacher over which Shakespeare play best represented a feminist portrayal of comedy, but you knew what feminism and comedy were defined as in your syllabus.

What you did not have (I hope!) were teachers openly arguing and criticising each other's views and ways of interpreting the works. This is not the case at university level. Academia thrives on disagreement; it is how new ideas come about, and universities are an incredible place of innovation, change, and fresh thinking. However, for those of us used to a right and wrong answer, this can be disconcerting.

You may be taught how to calculate the effect size by one lecturer one week and told how valuable this will be, only to be told the very same week by a different member of staff never to calculate the effect size as it is not a good measure and is a waste of your time. This is an extreme example, from my own experience, and many examples will not be this obvious; but there will be disagreements, especially in the social sciences and humanities. Even in the natural sciences this occurs. For example, in physics this may present as debates around theories, which, unlike laws, will have those who argue against them, or question their validity. So how do we disentangle the views and work out what is 'right'?

Firstly, we accept that there may not be a 'right', only a 'right for us', and that that may change several times over the course of our degree programme and our life. *And that's okay*. It's okay to change our minds; there is no point going to university if you come out the same as when you went in. Politicians are often criticised for making U-turns, or changing their minds on subjects, however, at university, this is encouraged as it shows flexibility of thinking.

Secondly, we listen to every idea that is presented to us. In my line of work, I read several articles a week whose premise I thoroughly disagree with, but I still read them. If someone has studied a topic to the level where they are teaching you and 400 other students about it, there will be something of value in what they say, even if you merely use it as a counter-argument in a paragraph where you play 'devil's advocate'.

Thirdly, we realise we may not have been told the whole truth before, especially in natural sciences. Much like at GCSE when they tell you how many electrons are in each shell of a particle, and then at A-Level they tell you a different number, degree-level studies may uncover several facts that are very different from those you were taught at school. This is due to the complexity of certain topics, and the emphasis on passing exams often means the deeper theories behind certain concepts are not fully explored. Even throughout your degree, some things may change. For example, the way light moves as a wave is commonly taught one way (Snell's Law) in the first year, and a different way (Fraunhofer/Fresnel approximations) in the third of fourth year. Be prepared for facts to change as you move up to degree level.

Finally – and this is a hard one to do – remember who is marking the work. We write for different purposes, and at university we write to communicate, to explore, and to pass exams. If your lecturer believes that effect-size calculations are a waste of time, including them in your assignment may not be the best use of your time. Lecturers like to know you have been listening to them, and so citing their work, their theories, and their ideas is a good way of demonstrating this. You are still entitled to your own opinion, and if you feel strongly about something, then by all means write it, just be prepared to back it up with references.

Academic opportunities

Your degree doesn't have to be limited to the lecture hall. There are dozens of opportunities to expand around and within your course, and these can be great for your personal development and future career prospects. Autistic people can often give themselves too many things to focus on and commit to, so ensure you do not get burnt out by all the additional opportunities and focus on what you would enjoy most, and what would be most beneficial to you and your future.

Placements and internships

You may already be on a sandwich course which includes a placement year, but there are also often opportunities to work over the summer as an intern for the university or the students' union. Often this will be in recruitment or curriculum design, or an academic might need a research assistant for a few weeks to help on a specific project. These are great opportunities to get more experience, keep busy, and earn a bit of money! Keep an eye out in your university emails and on their jobs portal for opportunities like this.

Year abroad

When applying for your course, you may have already applied for a course that has a year abroad, and therefore already be certain this is something you want to do. However, you may also decide in your first or second year that this is something you want to try, and some universities will allow you to apply for one and switch course. A year abroad is a fantastic opportunity to explore another culture, speak another language, and meet new people. It could also be very overwhelming, especially if you have only just adjusted to living away from home for the first time. My ethos is very much 'take every opportunity that comes your way' but with the caveat of: if it is best for you.

You may not want to go away for a year, and there is a lot of admin to complete in the process. Additionally, your friends may have finished their degrees by the time you return. These factors should not stop you from applying, but have a think about what is most important to you. Ultimately, a year abroad is one of the few times in your life when you can live in another country easily, without the life commitments that might come as you get older. If you think you might want to live abroad one day, do a year abroad while at university.

Being a representative for your course

I was the academic representative for my course throughout my degree, running unopposed for three years (it wasn't a particularly desirable role at my university) to be the go-between among the staff and students in my department. I enjoyed this position, and it gave me a sense of purpose and a feeling that I had an impact on the progression of the course. It also meant people relied on me and came to me with their problems; helping others had always been something I strived towards. It also allowed me to be involved in discussions about how to improve the course, as well as getting an insight into the statistics on course satisfaction and first-hand information on new modules etc. that might be coming our way. If you liked being on a student council or similar in the past, I would recommend putting yourself forwards for student representative.

Second year and beyond

People often say the second year is the worst of the three years of undergraduate study, and I think I would say this was true for me – academic demands are higher, and suddenly your grades count towards your final degree classification. You might have coasted through the first year using knowledge from your A-Levels, but now you are out of your depth. You might also start to realise that the 'best friends' you signed a house with back in the autumn of your first year are actually super annoying, and should stop using your milk, and maybe hoover once in a while. The novelty of being at university might have worn off, and suddenly things feel much harder.

There is no cure-all for the second-year blues, but using some of the mental and physical health advice in this book might help you overcome it slightly. Talking to others about how you are feeling and making a few visits home might help alleviate some of the stress. This is also a good time to take advantage of the counselling services offered to you by the university.

There are sometimes decisions you need to make in the second year about years abroad, placements, and what your dissertation will be on. Being organised and on the ball will stop everything feeling like it is coming at you at once. If you know you need to let your supervisor know what you want to do your dissertation on by May, set aside some time in March and April to consider your options and read around the subjects. If you want to apply for funding for postgraduate study, you will also need to factor this into the latter part of your second year, as deadlines are sometimes in the autumn/winter of the third year.

Chapter 8: What next after your degree?

You are coming towards the end of your undergraduate degree and starting to wonder where you want to go next. It is good to start thinking about this a year before the end of your degree, so the second year of a three-year course, or third year of a four-year one. It's not always an easy topic to think about; you will have come to see your university as home and made and lost many friends along the way. Moving away, and moving on, from that can be a form of grief in itself. It is also an exciting prospect, as you consider the next chapter in your life and the steps you will take along the way. As with all big decisions, take some time to consider your options – don't say yes to the first job offer you get just so you have somewhere to go after university. Equally, don't leave it until your graduation day to realise the money from your student loan has run out and you have nowhere to go come August. Jot down some ideas of what you want to do, where you would like to live, and how you will get there, and use the careers service at the university, as they can help you develop a plan, be it for work or further study.

Further study

Somewhere between a fifth and a quarter of undergraduate students choose to go on to postgraduate study, some of the most common are described here, but this list is not exhaustive. Postgraduate study is an excellent way to further your education and make yourself more employable. For me, it was a chance to explore a topic that I loved but didn't get to cover in depth at undergraduate.

However, it is worth noting that postgraduate degrees can be expensive if you do not have a studentship, and don't carry with them the same student finance grants and bursaries that undergraduate study does. For example, you can borrow around £12,000 through student finance currently, but this often will only cover the course fees and leaves nothing for maintenance to live off of while you study. Some master's degrees will be more than this amount, with an MBA potentially four, five, or even six times as much. Any postgraduate loans you take out will be in addition to your undergraduate loan, and you will need to pay them back at the same time, meaning bigger monthly payments once you get a job.

> **PGCert and PGCE:** Postgraduate certificates (PGCerts) are courses with fewer credits than a master's degree. A Postgraduate Certificate in Education (PGCE) is a teacher training course where you can gain Qualified Teacher Status (QTS), which allows you to teach in UK schools.

If you wish to train as a teacher, there are also other routes to do this, including undergraduate degrees with QTS, and train as you teach schemes where you get paid to work while you study. Look into these schemes carefully as they can be very intensive, and sometimes you have to pay back any money they give you if you choose to drop out or not go into teaching.

> **Master's degree:** Typically a one-year degree which is at the level above an undergraduate degree.

A master's degree is a great opportunity to explore a subject in more depth. However, you do not necessarily need to do a master's in the same subject you have just graduated with, so it can also be a great chance to learn about a different discipline. A lot of people use a master's to be able to meet certain professional standards, for example, a master's in business administration (MBA) is a highly sought-after qualification in the business world and will greatly open up job opportunities, although it usually clocks in as the most expensive degree out there. Some people might have their sights set on doctoral study, which usually requires a master's degree; these master's will need to include methods-based study relevant to your field as you will need these skills to begin a doctorate.

A lot of undergraduates talk about doing a 'panic master's', where they will do a master's because they are not ready to leave university, or they do not know what they want to do yet. If you can afford to do this, it can be a good way to give yourself more time to figure out what you want to do. However, a master's degree is hard work – it will be a big jump up from your undergraduate, so it is by no means an easy option out of the working world!

> **Graduate entry medicine:** For students with a relevant undergraduate degree, it is possible to go onto a graduate programme of study where you will qualify with a degree in medicine in a shorter time than an undergraduate degree in medicine would take.

> **Doctoral study:** Typically three or four years of full-time study above master's level, after which you can call yourself a doctor. There are different types, a PhD (Doctor of Philosophy) is the most common, but there are also EdD (Doctor of Education), and MD (Doctor of Medicine). Other doctorates exist, and other countries will have different names for doctorates also, but these are the most common.

A lot of Autistic people go on to study at doctoral level. The independence and being your own boss can appeal to those of us who never fit in in the school environment. However, doctorates are gruelling, lonely degrees, and not for the faint-hearted. You are the only person who will ever truly know what it is you are studying, which can make life difficult when you need support or advice. Make sure you have a good supervisor who can support you properly and knows about Autism and the difficulties Autistic people might face during a degree.

The world of work

Getting a job after university will feel very strange. Tiny things you never thought about, like being home for any parcels arriving, will become issues you need to overcome. Your time is no longer your own but is now controlled by an organisation. You must book time off for holidays, sometimes many months in advance. You might even need to start ironing your clothes again. However, you will get that wonderful thing at the end of the month: your first paycheck. You will probably have more money than you've had before, once your taxes, national insurance, pension, and union subscriptions have been taken off, and you've paid your rent and bills, of course.

Getting a job is a big change, but the regular hours, sense of structure, and new support mechanisms can be very helpful for Autistic people. If you're lucky and you get a job you really enjoy, with people you like, it won't even feel like work.

Job applications

When you apply for your first job, it can seem like a lot of work. You will probably need a CV, a cover letter, and other documentation. However, the upside is that once you have these prepared, they are fairly easy to modify for the next job you apply for. There are many CV templates out there, but make sure you tailor it to the job you are applying for. You might have been a line monitor in Year 6, but if you are applying for an apprenticeship at an accountancy firm, they might want to know about your role as treasurer of the rowing society instead. Ensure you don't repeat yourself too much in your cover letter; they will be able to see that you got a 2:1 in history, so focus on the skills you developed during your degree and how these will make you a good candidate for the role. Say what you love about their company, what accomplishments they have made in their field, and why you would love to work for them.

> **Imposter syndrome:** When someone doubts their own talents, abilities or accomplishments; they may feel like they are a fraud and that someone will expose them as such.

It can be hard selling yourself, especially when you are fresh out of university and may not feel like you are good enough for the roles you are applying for. This can be a case of **imposter syndrome**, and you can fight it by reading the criteria for the job. If you meet all the essential criteria then you are most certainly good enough for this job!

References

Much like with your UCAS application, you will need references for job applications. These are needed firstly to make sure you are who you say you are, but also to give you character assessments, for example you were always on time and eager in lectures. The jobs you apply for after university will not expect you to necessarily have had a previous employer, so you can often put down academic staff as your reference. This could be a leader for a module you particularly enjoyed, or your personal tutor/ academic adviser. Make sure you ask your referees beforehand if they are okay to give you a reference. Academic staff receive many reference requests and if they aren't expecting them, or do not recognise your name, they may well just delete the email. You can also ask staff from any summer jobs, part-time work, or work experience to give you a reference, and the same applies that you need to ask them in advance.

An example email for academic staff can be found below:

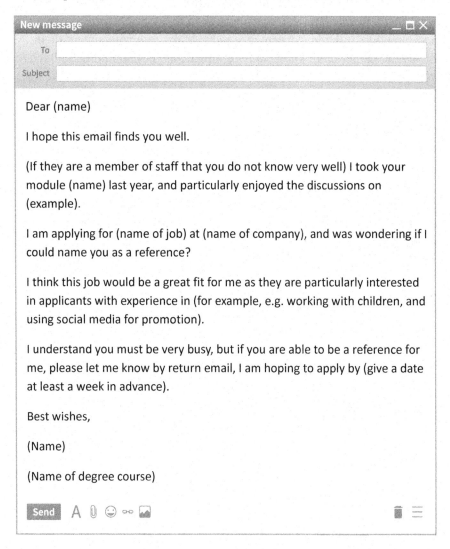

New message

To

Subject

Dear (name)

I hope this email finds you well.

(If they are a member of staff that you do not know very well) I took your module (name) last year, and particularly enjoyed the discussions on (example).

I am applying for (name of job) at (name of company), and was wondering if I could name you as a reference?

I think this job would be a great fit for me as they are particularly interested in applicants with experience in (for example, e.g. working with children, and using social media for promotion).

I understand you must be very busy, but if you are able to be a reference for me, please let me know by return email, I am hoping to apply by (give a date at least a week in advance).

Best wishes,

(Name)

(Name of degree course)

Send

Assessment centres

You might have thought your university exams were the last ones you would ever take, however some graduate jobs hold massive assessment centre days, with exams, group work and interviews. These can take place over one day, or even over a few days, and assess a wide range of skills including communication, leadership and decision making. You will be observed and assessed throughout the day by managers and human resources (HR) staff, who will judge your performance based on the whole day. These can be very intense experiences, especially for Autistic people, and you may need to go to several before you are accepted due to the low acceptance rates. Make sure you contact them in advance to let them know you are Autistic as they should be judging you on your ability to do the job, not on how well you communicate in a 'neurotypical' way.

Job interviews

My advice here is similar to the advice for university interviews: be prepared, do your research, dress the part. Job interviews can be scary and you may need to go to lots of them before you land a job, so it can feel repetitive. However, it is important to treat every one like it is your dream job, at your dream company, as this will give you the energy you need to come across well.

Always have a question to ask them at the end, which shows you are keen and inquisitive. Save the more controversial questions you might have, such as what they are doing to close their gender pay gap, and ask about their line mana ger system, or a certain project they are working on right now.

Access to Work

This government scheme, run in England, Wales and Scotland (for Northern Ireland, see indirect: Employment Support Information), is aimed at helping disabled people get into work and to maintain careers. You may not identify with the label 'disabled', but this is the phrase used to include Autism for this service. You can also get Access to Work support for health conditions including mental health conditions such as depression and anxiety. It is a self-referral service you can use once you have a job, and it is best to apply for it before you start work, to make sure everything is in place before you start. The process can take a few weeks, so if you get your job in May, to start in September, it is best to apply in May.

Once you have referred yourself, you will have an assessment to discuss what would be useful for you. It is useful to have a list written down already which you can refer to. There is a template at the back of this book. Much like with DSA, you will not necessarily get everything you ask for, and they will not fund **reasonable adjustments** (things your workplace should be doing anyway).

Supports Autistic people may find useful:

- An adjustable desk which you can sit or stand at, to help if you fidget a lot.
- Ergonomic desk set-up.
- Autism training for your line manager.
- Specialist counselling.
- A specialist workplace coach.
- A support worker to help with admin tasks and organising.
- Text-to-speech software, or speech-to-text software.
- A tablet that can turn written words into text.
- Screen tinters, or glasses to change the colour of the screen glare.
- Funds so someone can travel with you to conferences for support.

This list is not exhaustive, and it can be useful to discuss support with your manager before you apply, as they may think of extra things that could be good to request. Visit the Access to Work webpages for up-to-date information on this scheme.

Occupational health

You may have already encountered occupational health if you have undertaken a degree with a practical element, such as teacher training. The role of occupational health staff is to ensure people can undertake their occupation in a way that doesn't cause harm to their health or well-being. This can include things like making sure people are sitting correctly at their desks so as to reduce back and neck injuries. Before you start a job, you may have a discussion with an occupational health team member, who may want to discuss how being Autistic might impact your job role. This can feel invasive, but they are not trying to catch you out so as to take away your job offer, they are mostly just creating a risk assessment for each staff member, so they are aware of the challenges each person faces. Be honest during your meeting, and they may help you to develop some ideas for reasonable adjustments in your workplace.

Graduate jobs

One of the most common jobs for someone to take after their undergraduate degree is finished is a graduate job, which just means you need a degree to start it. Graduate schemes are popular as they combine work and training, and often have a guaranteed permanent job at the end. These are essential for certain careers, especially in accounting and finance and similar fields. Graduate jobs and schemes are likely to require assessment centres and interviews, as demand is very high. Many employers will also advertise at your university quite heavily, and certain companies will be deemed much more desirable than others due to their brand or the benefits they offer. Consider your choices carefully and read the small print; for example many graduate schemes require you to work for them for a certain number of years after you have completed the scheme. If your graduate scheme is three years, and you must work for them for five years after you finish, you are committing to eight years of your life when you sign that contract, so be sure that this is what you want.

Sabbatical officers

If you have been involved in the students' union or college at your university, you might consider taking a sabbatical year after your undergraduate degree. While the term usually means someone who takes a break from work, in terms of universities in the UK, a sabbatical officer is someone who takes up a one-year post to work at the students' union or similar. These people are often elected by the student body, and are paid, and sometimes also given accommodation at the university. Roles might include the president of the students' union, sports officers, or welfare officers. If you think this is something you might want to do, get involved early, as you are more likely to be considered, and elected, if you have lots of experience engaging with students and organising activities.

Academic jobs

If, like me, you never want to leave the world of academia and learning, there are many jobs within universities that you can apply for. These offer the familiarity of the university environment with the independence of the workplace and can be very Autistic-friendly. Research jobs allow you to delve even further into topics you find interesting, as well as design your own projects and add your own entry into the book of knowledge.

If you want to work at a university but do not want to teach or do research, student support jobs can help you to support those who need extra help at university – maybe you can offer them the help you found useful while you were an undergraduate or the help you wished you'd had. There are also jobs in administration and recruitment which can appeal to those with organisational skills and a good customer-facing manner.

A 'post-doc' is a job for someone who has just finished a PhD. They are similar to graduate jobs in that they often involve further training, and are on shorter-term contracts, rather than a permanent basis.

Belated gap year

Many people choose to take a break after university, including many Autistic people who feel burnt out after an intense degree with lots of demands on their academic and social lives. Some take the time to travel and see a bit more of the world before they choose somewhere to settle down into a job. If you can afford to do so, taking a break is a valid choice, and can allow you time to consider where you want to go next. For Autistic people especially, if your degree has not been an overly positive experience, a year or so without studying or working full-time can allow the body and mind to 'reset'. This is, of course, not an option for everybody, and many people will need to go straight into work in order to sustain themselves and/or others who depend on them.

Chapter 9: Advice for parents and carers

So, your young person is off to university. This is a big moment for any parent or carer, but even more so for parents who have witnessed their child experience more challenges and barriers than others. You might think they seem too young to be going off to university and wonder if you seemed that young when you left home. You might wonder how an 18-year-old is even an adult… It should be at least 25! While they are thinking about their lectures and what friends they will make, you might be thinking about whether they will be eating their greens (they won't) and whether will they call home (yes, especially if they need money).

The good news is that university will likely be a very positive experience where they can explore their independence, try new things, meet new people, and delve deeper into a specific subject that they have a passion for. However, they may also face a whole new set of challenges, and you won't be by their side this time, so preparing them now can help them cope with the trials and changes ahead of them. Talking about and reflecting on your own time at university, if you went, can be helpful here. Consider the following questions:

- What did you look forward to the most about university?
- What was the biggest surprise after starting university?
- How often did you call home?
- What did you wish you'd known before starting?

You don't need to share these answers with anyone, but it might help you advise your young person if you jog your memory for how you felt in their shoes. Even if you didn't attend university, think about when you left home: what did it feel like and what support did you wish you'd had?

Finally, remember you're not just preparing them for going to university: you're preparing yourself. This isn't just about their experience, you're about to face a huge change too, and it's okay to think about that and to feel strong emotions.

What you can do to help

You may feel a bit helpless as they make their choices, as although you can tell them what you think is best for them, at the end of the day, that choice is theirs alone. However, there are many things you can do to help their transition as smooth as possible and help them achieve the goal of attending university.

Applying

Attend open days! If you can afford to and can take the time off work, take your young person to open days to see lots of universities. This can be a real bonding time for you both; I remember going with my dad to one, and as the tour guide showed us round mouldy accommodation blocks and the rubbish-strewn campus, we locked eyes and both agreed 'Definitely not here!' It is a chance to see new towns and cities together and get a feel of what they are looking for in a university. Even if it's not their top choice, it can be worth going along to get an idea of what a university looks like.

It can be tempting to apply to a university because your best friend is going, but, if possible, make sure your young person is applying for themselves, not for who will be going with them. Friendships are likely to change, evolve and develop, and those students may not even get their first-choice university anyway. Ensure your young person can justify their reasons for why they picked each university beyond who else in their class is applying there.

Considering future career options is important, as some degrees will lead straight into jobs while others are more competitive areas of work. However, employability shouldn't be the only reason for taking a degree, and if they don't enjoy it, they will not do as well, increasing the likelihood of failure or drop-out. Discuss where they would like to be in five or ten years, and which degree course might help them get there. At the end of the day, though, it is their decision where to go, and your role is to help them get there. Just make sure they have an insurance choice with lower grades than their firm choice (see p.31), and keep your fingers crossed for results day!

Familiarise yourself with the system

Make sure you're up to date with the lingo around university applications. If you went to university, you may be familiar with some of the process, but you may not have used the UCAS system as it is, so take advantage of online resources and any talks your young person's school/college puts on. Being able to understand what they are talking about when they discuss their **'firm'** and **'insurance'** choices will help you to support them in making decisions so that they don't feel alone in these big life choices. Talk to other parents and carers to get an idea of where other students are in their journey, but remember your young person is on their own path, so shouldn't judge themselves by what everyone else is doing.

As they head off to university, it can be good to also swot up on common phrases like **'summative'** and **'formative'**, so you can (hopefully!) congratulate them on their results when they let you know. Make a big deal when they achieve good grades, and ask them how their studies are going regularly, but not too often as to stress them out if they're falling behind. You might not be able to support them academically, as it is unlikely they are studying a subject you are very familiar with, but you can always offer to be a proofreader for spelling mistakes in essays and stay available as a sounding board for ideas.

Cooking

Your young person might be going into catered halls, which means they won't have the pressure of cooking for themselves. However, if they plan

to live outside of catered halls at some point, or if they are going into self-catered halls, you may want to go through some cooking basics with them. You can't stop them eating chicken nuggets every night, or ordering pizza at 2am, but you can teach them these basics for when they feel like branching out. A rotation for five or so meals works well; teach them their favourite meals, or simplified versions for those low-energy days. Using the freezer is a fantastic way to help them eat healthily by batch cooking and storing pre-prepared vegetables. See the cooking section in this book for more tips.

Avoid buying them all the smart cooking tools and gadgets as they are unlikely to use them. Unless they currently use the toastie-maker every day, they won't when they're at university. Focus instead on helping them learn how to prepare common fruit and vegetables such as onions, potatoes, tomatoes and carrots. Teach them the shelf life of perishables like eggs, meat and bread. Knife skills and safety when handling hot items are important, as is reminding them never to cook while intoxicated. I have seen too many injuries caused by undergraduates thinking they have knife dexterity or heatproof hands after coming home from a night out.

Finally, on behalf of all university staff everywhere, please teach them that metal does not go in the microwave.

Finances

They will hopefully already have a bank account, but it is also important to discuss budgeting. If they are fully funded through student finance, recommend to them that they give themselves a weekly allowance of between £50-£100 (London may be towards the more expensive end) for shopping, going out, and anything else they might need. If you are financially supporting them, discuss with them how this will work and budget for this yourself, remembering that if you have multiple children it will need to be the same amount for each of them in the future too. I recommend weekly or monthly payments rather than lump sums, as this can help them to budget on a smaller scale.

Discuss financial planning, savings accounts and interest rates, and make sure they get their student bank account as soon as they can (after they have their confirmation of a place from the university). As discussed more fully below, talk to them about lending money to friends, and how to spot if someone is taking advantage of them. It is also important to discuss how to recognise scams and the dangers of gambling and placing bets.

Friendships, relationships and staying safe

Going off to university holds a great deal of excitement for many at the prospect of new friendships, new people to meet, and possible romantic opportunities. Equally, these prospects can also cause anxiety in Autistic young people, through fear of the uncertain or unexpected, and through worries of acting in the wrong way or saying the wrong thing. You can help by reassuring them that they will have lots of opportunities to meet new people, but that not everyone will end up being their friend.

Overall, the chances of finding people you get on with are much higher at university than in the small school/college environment; there are clubs tailored to specific special interests, and you will encounter different people in each lecture and seminar. All this may be overwhelming, and it is important to remind young people they do not need to meet their best friends for life during their first week/term/year at university.

Autistic people can develop very strong bonds with others very quickly, and this is especially the case when young people are living in close proximity, such as sharing a flat. One thing I could have benefitted from was being reminded to 'take it slow' with friendships. Don't sign up for a house for second year with the first person they get on with, and don't get into a serious relationship with someone before they have found their feet on their own.

When it comes to relationships, *talk about sex*. This can be abstract – talk about how important it is for people to stay safe to avoid contracting STIs or unplanned pregnancies. Show them how to use a condom if they haven't done this at school, and give them a box to take with them; even if they aren't sexually active themselves, they might be able to help someone else.

Talk about consent. Unfortunately, it is sadly the case that Autistic people, especially Autistic women and girls, are often victims of crimes such as sexual assault and rape and are more likely to experience domestic abuse and be in unhealthy or unsafe relationships. Talk about what is normal and healthy in a relationship, and that you should always be able to say no if you are uncomfortable in any situation, not just sexual ones. Let them know who they can go to at the university if they need help or advice – this could be the counselling service, the welfare team, or security staff.

Unfortunately, Autistic people can often become victims of mate crime, where someone will exploit their desire to fit in and have friends in order to take advantage of them. It is very hard to tell someone that the person they believe to be a close friend or partner is using or exploiting them, so the most important thing you can do is to discuss what healthy friendships and relationships look like, and how to set boundaries with people. Teaching practices like not lending money to friends and how you should take turns buying rounds at the bar, can help to model what healthy friendships are. At universities, **hazing** is becoming less common, but can still present a huge issue, when students are made to do things they are not comfortable with. Impress upon your young person the importance of **consent** in all areas of life, be it posting a photo of someone online without them knowing, buying someone a double when they asked for a single, or being told to down a bottle of wine so they can join the football team.

> **Mate crime:** When a perpetrator pretends to befriend a victim in order to exploit them financially, physically or sexually.

As well as talking about safe sex and healthy relationships, consider talking to them about how to maintain positive mental health while at university. Developing and keeping positive habits is hard for the best of us, even more so when you are away from home for the first time, talk about staying active, taking time to rest, and talking to someone about your feelings. Staying safe physically is important too, so make sure they have had all their vaccinations, and know when to go to the doctor or pharmacist if they are unwell.

It can be hard for lots of parents and carers, going from being able to know when your young person is unwell, to drive them to the doctor and know every detail of their lives, to suddenly being cut off. You will have no access to the young person's health or academic records, and the university will not be able to discuss your young person with you. This is a difficult part of the transition to deal with, and while the young person will be celebrating their new-found independence, you may be mourning the loss of their childhood and any control you had over their safety and well-being. Keep in touch with them, but respect their privacy, and this will make them more likely to come to you if

Have plans

When you drop them off, it may seem like a long time until you see them again; it may well be the longest you have ever gone apart since they've lived with you. They may also be worrying about this, even through the excitement of starting university. For both of you, therefore, it is important to have a fixed date in place for when you will next see each other. This

could be in December at the end of their first term, or a weekend's visit in three weeks' time, or a video call at 5pm on Monday after their first day of lectures. Having something in the diary gives you a fixed point to look forward to when things get hard, and they need an anchor to home. When you call them, you can say 'and I'll see you in two weeks' before you end the call. These events in the calendar where you will spend time together will keep that bond and that connection, and give you both something to look forward to.

Saying goodbye

Because my university was so far from home, my parents stayed in a local hotel after driving me up. This meant we could go out for dinner the night before they drove back up. I decided I didn't want to see them again in the morning, however, as I wanted to start university on my own terms. Ask your young person what they would prefer; some might want you close for the first 24 hours, although this may make it difficult when you eventually leave. Going out for dinner or a coffee before you leave can help them to settle in, and means they are exploring the local area.

Take them for their first shop if you can, this means you can make sure they aren't just buying frozen pizzas and sambuca, but also means they can get some staples in before they have to worry about paying for everything themselves! It is also good, if you have a car, to take them to do their first shop, as you can fit more in, especially if you are buying bedding, kitchenware, or anything they need that their room doesn't have such as a waste-paper bin.

Hide a little gift in one of their bags – a book, picture, or photo album – that they can find when they arrive. Or slip it into one of the drawers in their new room; they can open it once you've left and be reminded that you are still there for them, even if you aren't physically in the same space.

When it comes to keeping in touch, try and be led by them, drop them a text every week or so if you haven't heard from them, but let them come to you. If it helps to have a consistent time in the diary, and they want regular calls, set a time aside to video chat once a week or fortnight to keep in touch. You may find your relationship improves once they are at university, and you will be able to begin your relationship with them as an independent adult for the first time, rather than reminding them to pick their socks up off the floor and bring down their dirty plates from their room.

What you might feel

Be proud

Be proud of them for how far they've come and how many obstacles they've overcome to get to university. And be proud of yourself – you helped them get here.

Allow yourself to be sad

It is a big change, and the end of a chapter. Your child, who has faced so many struggles, who you have probably watched more closely and carefully than if they had not been Autistic, is leaving to make their own way in the world. Yes, they'll be back at Christmas with a suitcase full of unwashed clothes, and yes, they might even call to let you know how they're doing. But it's still okay to be sad. When you get home to that quiet bedroom, with the bedclothes stripped from the bed, sit down, look at the walls with the pictures, revision notes, and certificates stuck to them, stick on ABBA's 'Slipping Through My Fingers' and have a cry. It's okay. Order yourself a takeaway and watch some mindless television, because these feelings of grief are normal, and they will pass.

Chapter 10: Advice for educators

The following chapter will include some best practices from other universities, as well as some Autistic voices and what they found helpful at university. Understanding and acceptance of Autism are increasing every year, especially since the introduction of the Autism Act in 2009. However, many misconceptions still exist, and the low life expectancy and low levels of well-being among the Autistic community are a significant worry. Autistic people are more likely to experience poor physical and mental health and are especially prone to depression and anxiety stemming from feeling out of place in a society not built for them. In your role as an educator, you can help Autistic people to be ready for university, and to support them once they are at university.

What is Autism?

'Autism is a neurological difference mainly affecting social communication and interaction. Many Autistic people have co-occurring diagnoses including anxiety and ADHD. Autistic people have numerous strengths; these include honesty, loyalty, passion for a particular area and creativity.'

Lauren Smith, *Autistic student in Autism studies*

At its simplest, Autism is characterised by difficulties interacting with and understanding non-Autistic people, experiencing sensory difficulties such as not liking bright lights or loud noises, and enjoying repetitive activities or foods. It is a difference in the way someone's brain works, and the diagnosis has changed a lot over the last half a century since it was first introduced into diagnostic manuals.

In recent years, the neurodiversity movement has grown; this movement, originally focused on Autism but now includes other neurological differences such as ADHD, characterises Autism as a natural human variation not in need of treatment. This movement grew out of the social model of disability, which situates disability as a fault of society for not adapting to its individuals, rather than blaming the individuals for not adapting to society. In practice, this would mean it is the owners of the building without a ramp that are disabling the person who cannot enter the building in their wheelchair, rather than the person in the chair.

Identity is very important to people, and having an appreciation of the individual terms one person uses to describe themselves is important. The majority of Autistic people prefer to **use identity-first** language to describe themselves (definition in the glossary), and using this language in webpages, documents and policies at your workplace will signal to others that you have an inclusive space. However, if an Autistic person states that they prefer a different language, it is important to honour this for that person, as you would with any identity.

Autistic people often have poorer mental health than non-Autistic people, and this is important to remember when setting up support. Sadly, rates of suicide are much higher in the Autistic population than in the general population, with the greatest risk in women and those with co-occurring intellectual disability. Social isolation, lack of support and difficulties managing intrusive and repetitive thoughts are all thought to contribute to this higher risk in Autistic people. Ongoing **masking** has also been linked to a higher risk of suicidal thoughts, so ensuring Autistic people can be their authentic selves is paramount. For more advice and support on mental health and suicidality in Autistic people, see the National Autistic Society's website.

Misconceptions

'Asperger's syndrome is "Autism lite".'

Asperger's syndrome was a form of Autism diagnosis between 1994 and 2013, the main difference between Asperger's and Autism diagnoses was for an Asperger's diagnosis, the child needed to have had no delay in speech and language. It did not mean anyone was more or less Autistic than someone with an Autism diagnosis, however, it led many to believe that those with Asperger's were 'gifted savants', due to some portrayals in the media. The term was removed and has fallen out of favour due to this false dichotomy, but also due to evidence linking Hans Asperger (whom the syndrome was named after) to the Nazi party. You may still have some students who, like me, have a historical Asperger's diagnosis. Their diagnosis does not change, but it is now under one umbrella of Autism, rather than two separate diagnoses.

'You can catch Autism.'

I never know where to begin with this one, except to point people towards the overwhelming, proven, scientific evidence that environmental factors, such as vaccines or eating blue Smarties, do not cause Autism. We are currently in the midst of several measles outbreaks across the UK, as those who were unvaccinated during the time when lies were being spread around vaccines, have grown up and started attending university, or are even having children of their own. When I worked at the university, we had an outbreak of mumps which no number of silly selfies showing how big their mumps are making up for the fact it can cause infertility and other long-term health conditions. Lies and misinformation can cost lives. Take time to educate yourself and those around you on these important topics.

'Autistic people are all good at maths.'

This is a common one I hear, and as I struggle through the statistics I need to complete for work, I wish this were true. While many people may excel in mathematics, it is not a trait of Autism.

'Autistic people play the victim.'

Feelings of persecution were once actually labelled as part of the diagnostic criteria in early iterations of Autism diagnoses. However, the truth is that Autistic people are more likely to be victims. These feelings of persecution are often very real and should be taken seriously. Unfortunately, Autistic people are significantly more likely to be the victims of mate crime, domestic abuse and sexual assault. Nine out of ten Autistic women will face sexual violence compared to 30% of the general population. Always believe the person in front of you.

'More people are Autistic these days.'

Statistically, this is true. Rates of diagnosis have risen, and where the rate used to be 1 in 10,000, it is now as high as 1 in 36. However, whether this actually represents *a rise in Autistic people* is another question. It wasn't always a diagnosis, and then when it did become one, there were very few people trained to diagnose it. Furthermore, the diagnosis has changed over the years, with some symptoms being removed, and others added. People didn't used to believe women and girls could be Autistic, or that adults were Autistic, believing instead that it was a condition of childhood. Many over 60s are now receiving diagnoses for Autism, a diagnosis that didn't even exist when they were children.

What schools can do

To prepare your Autistic students for university, there is much more than merely the academic side of things to consider. This will be a massive transition for them, and the earlier you can start to introduce strategies to help the transition the better. University visits are a great way for students to see and experience university life, within the safety of a school trip with school staff. Doing this at the beginning of Year 12/Lower Sixth helps to frame the next two years in terms of what comes next for those who are planning to go to university. university residentials, talks from university staff, and early discussions about future plans will help students to think about where they want to go next.

In terms of applying for university, Autistic students may want to start earlier than their non-Autistic peers. Supporting students by having clear deadlines and frequent reminders of them will help them produce quality applications without feeling stressed. However, be sure not to fall into the trap of talking about university non-stop, as this may overwhelm students, as well as alienate those who do not wish to go to university.

Alongside applications for universities, DSA, and student finance, it is important to consider the other aspects of leaving school. Managing money is a topic of conversation all students should have before they leave school, including creating and sticking to budgets, as well as how loans work: specifically, the sort of loan they will have e.g. Student Finance England.

Do:

- Start talking about university as soon as possible.
- Organise trips to universities.
- Allow Autistic students to start their applications early.
- Have clear deadlines for all stages of applications.
- Discuss practical elements of post-school life such as cooking and finances.

Don't:

- Assume an Autistic person can't/won't want to attend university.
- Only talk about university.

How you can help with the transition

Arrange for your Autistic students to have additional one-to-ones to discuss their transition, including their parents or carers if the Autistic person wishes, and you think it would be useful. In these meetings, talk about what their plans are, and what transition support they would like. If you have mental health support at your school, consider setting up sessions for your Autistic students in the final year of their study so that they have a space to discuss any exam stress and worries for the years ahead.

'Once I had made [my university] decisions, my school contacted my local university and booked some transition days, which enabled me to visit the campus with a teacher from school and walk around to familiarise myself with the environment. The next step was to meet some of the lecturers and choose where I would like to sit in the different lecture halls and classrooms and any other adjustments I might need.'

Sophia Christophi, *Autistic psychology student*

For Sophia's full account, see pp.47-48. These transition visits can be highly useful and will give the Autistic student a better idea of where they are heading. It will also help them to focus on their exams, as they have a clearer, more attainable goal to work towards.

Social and practical issues of attending university should also be considered for all students, not just the Autistic ones. While sex education will have been covered in the lower years of school, it is never too late to recap before they go to university, along with some advice about drinking and drugs. Spiking is becoming an increasing issue across the country, so consider having a class on how to protect yourself from being spiked and what to do if you worry you have been spiked (see p.105 for more details). Preparing them also extends to reminding them to have their meningitis vaccination, and checking they are up to date with other jabs such as the MMR, especially as rates are at a historic low and university is a breeding ground for germs and viruses.

Things to consider for transitions:

- Visits to universities.
- Looking around where lectures and seminars will take place and halls of residence.
- Support meetings focused on transitions.
- Mental health counselling.
- Sex education recap.
- Alcohol and drugs education.
- Remind them to get vaccinated!

What universities can do

Based on 2020/21 Higher Education Statistics Agency (HESA) statistics, around 15% of students in higher education have a known disability. For the year ending December 2020, the Office for National Statistics estimated around 17.6% of 16 to 19-year-olds were Autistic. Disabled, and specifically Autistic, students make up a significant proportion of the UK higher education population of students, and it is therefore important that practitioners and educators are aware of Autism and how to best support Autistic students while at university.

While researching for this book, I contacted 90 universities across the UK, asking them what support was available for Autistic students starting at their institution, and 24 replied. Many merely signposted me to generic web pages, however some gave useful and detailed information on the Autism services they offer. These have been grouped into sections below and should give you some ideas of things that could be implemented at your own institution.

Open days

Nearly all the universities mentioned their open-day provision for Autistic students, with most mentioning they have a member of student services, inclusion, or welfare services on hand to speak to students and answer questions. Special talks on inclusion are run by some staff, with some having Autistic members of staff speak about their own experiences. Disabled student allowance (DSA) advice was also on offer from trained staff in the disability support services. Quiet spaces were also set aside for prospective students during open days. Some mentioned that they run alternative, quieter, open days, or open-day hours, for Autistic students, where the campus is quieter and calmer. Virtual tours were also available.

Student peer-support groups and societies, run through the university or students' union, were also present at some of these open days, and for the one-to-one tours, student ambassadors with knowledge of Autism accommodations such as avoiding busy areas were paired with Autistic prospective students.

Transition support

Support with transition starts early for some universities, with one offering introduction to higher education sessions and a course for local Autistic students starting in September of Year 13; this course aims to help prepare students for the transition to higher education, as well as recognise the skills they already have that will be useful for university, and helping them build new skills.

Many offer campus visits with tours over the summer before the student starts. One university mentioned the importance of offering several visits, as Autistic students can become overwhelmed easily. On these tours, some students are able to see the actual room they would be staying in. Full transition summer schools are also on offer, which are sometimes run in the weeks before the other students arrive.

Transition days were mentioned by some, offered by the inclusions and disability services to new students. These take place in person and online for Autistic students and include talks from disability services, a disability mentor, an accommodation staff member, and an academic talking about the difference between A-Levels and higher education, and explaining who to talk to if they need academic support. There are also question-and-answer sessions for Autistic students.

To assist with the transition once the students arrived at university, some universities have one-to-one transitional support assistants or orientation support for the first few weeks of term, as well as fast-track enrolment for Autistic students and a quiet space for them to complete this. Others have quiet tours of the campus for small groups and a chance to meet with their new specialist mentor. Below, Autistic contributor Lauren talks about her ideas for managing transitions at university.

'Micro and macro transitions can be incredibly daunting and anxiety-provoking for Autistic people. Starting university can be a huge leap into the unknown. The unique challenges of independent living, socialising, and taking care of mental health must not be underestimated; these are key areas where Autistic people may require additional, targeted support. An Autism-specific open day at the university and tours of student accommodation could be helpful so that people can begin to build like-minded connections and familiarise themselves with the support available. Sharing of information is crucial. Autistic people should be provided with opportunities to explain their strengths, challenges and needs with university staff; their preferred method of communication must be respected when they are expressing themselves. Additionally, regular meetings with disability and well-being teams and one-to-one mentoring should be offered as part of the Disabled Student's Allowance. It could also be helpful for staff to work with Autistic students to create a set of coping cards to help them navigate different situations.'

Lauren Smith, *Autistic student in Autism studies*

Orientation sessions

Some universities offer one-to-one or small group tours for Autistic students, where a member of staff from the support services or inclusion team can show them round outside of an open-day environment, and answer any questions the student might have. These are often offered outside of term time, in the summer, when staff have more time and the campus is quieter. One university combined this orientation tour with a chance for the students to talk one to one with a member of staff from their course, with the option for this to be done remotely via webinar also.

Pre-arrival information

One university sent me two very helpful leaflets that they send out to Autistic students, and students can also access them while at university. The first is aimed just at Autistic students and discusses things they can do before they arrive at university, how they can access help to get a diagnosis if they do not have one, and how to apply for DSA, as well as what support is available to students throughout their studies. There are QR codes, social media links, and contact details on the PDF also. The second PDF is for all students, and consists purely of QR codes to webpages on:

- Advice: council tax, extension requests and extenuating circumstances, support for care leavers, and support for carers.

- Mental health and well-being: concern about another student, counselling services, emergency information, local and national support, support when you are in crisis, and a well-being site.

- Funding: bursaries, learning funds and DSA.

- Accessibility: mental health support, and support for those with learning differences, and for Autistic students.

- Health: what to do if you are ill, registering with a GP, and getting vaccinated.

One-to-one support

Many universities mentioned that they offer one-to-one support for Autistic students, including:

- Specialist study skills tutors.
- Autism specialist mentors.
- DSA-funded mentors.
- Dedicated widening participation careers adviser.
- Disability coaches.
- Counselling.

They mentioned specifically how useful Autism specialist mentors and advisers can be for helping Autistic students manage their time and organisation, as well as being a point of contact for all aspects of university life. Offering one-to-one sessions regularly, sometimes weekly, as well as drop-in services, is favoured by universities because students can choose how they wish to access the service.

Support plans

Having a detailed support plan is encouraged by universities, some providing this for prospective students as well as current students. These plans include the students' reasonable adjustments for study, as well as staff liaising with the accommodation teams. Sometimes these plans have been developed by specialist advisers alongside students, and sometimes through the collaboration of departments.

Academic support

Universities highlighted how they provide academic staff with information regarding inclusion and disability and advice on how to accommodate Autistic students. This includes universities offering:

- Reading lists provided well in advance.
- Support workers during classes.
- Lecture recordings provided to students.
- Extra time and rest breaks in exams.
- Use of a PC for exams.
- Academic peer mentoring.

Freshers' week events

Early access to freshers' fairs was offered by some, although often arranged by the students' union rather than the university support services. This often takes place as a 'quiet hour' before the rest of the new students started. One university stated their students' union had a buddy system, where a student could go to societies they wanted to try with another student, so they did not have to try them out on their own. Alternative freshers' events that are quieter, such as board games and crafts events, are also offered to Autistic students.

Quiet spaces

Many of the universities that replied mentioned that they provide quiet spaces for students, some of which were located in the library as quiet study spaces specifically for Autistic or disabled students, whereas others are dotted around the campus. The ones in the libraries tended to have computers with assisted technology on them. Several quiet rooms had sensory toys, board games, a fidget toys in them, and one university stated they had a dedicated sensory room. Most of these quiet rooms are accessible to prospective students on open days also.

Diagnosis assistance

Students are offered support while they are obtaining a diagnosis, and one university even stated that they offer diagnostic assessments with an external provider, with student financial contribution.

DSA support

As many services are funded through **Disabled Students Allowance (DSA)**, universities offer support to students to apply for this if they did not already have it when they arrived. Some also provide interim support for students while they are waiting for their DSA to come through.

Mental health support

In addition to the counselling and mental health support available to all students, some universities highlight Autism-specific counselling and special mental health assistance programmes for those with additional needs. One university detailed an app that is available to all students with which they can request first aid and mental health support on campus, live chat, and can share their location if they need urgent support.

Moving in early

Many universities replied that they offer Autistic students the chance to move in early. This varies from earlier in the morning on the first day of freshers' week, a few days before, or up to two weeks before. The most common response was two or three days earlier than the other students. For some universities, this is done on a case-by-case basis while others offer it to all Autistic students.

Accommodation

Several universities stated that Autistic students have the option to live in halls for the duration of their course. Others mentioned subsidies, rent rebates, and funding made available to fund Autistic students to have en-suite accommodation or a studio room. Some universities have specific quiet halls. While in university accommodation, one university mentioned a residence welfare team who can help students if they are struggling with noise, socialising, or feelings of belonging, and run events, including some which are quiet and have minimal sensory overwhelm.

Peer support

Most universities explained what peer support their university offers, with some of these facilitated through student support services while others are organised by the students' union. Some of these are purely social clubs, meeting every week or fortnight either in person or remotely, whereas others are more formal peer support and mentoring. Many of these societies and groups have webpages from which students can find the contact details of the person in charge, social media handles, and the dates and times of any meetings. These groups hold discussions, go out for dinner, do puzzles, play board games, and do arts and crafts. Some are led by students while others are led by specialist Autism advisers and support service staff. Details of how to set up your own peer support group at your university can be found later in this chapter.

Webpages

In addition to the Autism peer support, clubs and societies webpages already mentioned, many universities have their own webpages dedicated to Autistic students. These show them where they can access support, awareness campaigns, and articles from Autistic students and staff, or about the achievements of Autistic students at the university. For some universities, this is a subsection of their 'disabled students' webpages, whereas others have entirely separate pages or even a whole website. For examples, see the resources section at the end of the book.

Summary of current practice at UK universities

- Support staff on hand at open days.
- Alternative quieter open-day events.
- Quiet spaces at open days.
- Transition summer schools and days.
- Transition support.
- Orientation sessions.
- Pre-arrival information leaflets.
- One-to-one support.
- Academic support.
- Exam adjustments.
- Quiet spaces.
- Diagnosis assistance.
- Early access to freshers' fairs.
- DSA application support.
- Mental health support.
- Early move in.
- Option to live in halls for the duration of the course.
- En-suite or studio accommodation funding.
- Quiet residences.
- Residence welfare teams.
- Quiet events.
- Peer support.
- Support plans.
- Dedicated Autism webpages.

Accommodations and reasonable adjustments

I was never a fan of the phrase 'reasonable adjustments', as I have never met an Autistic person asking for an unreasonable adjustment. No Autistic person that I know of is asking for a candyfloss machine to be installed in the back of every lecture hall, or for Bruce Springsteen to play on repeat at every formal dinner, great as both these things would be. No, Autistic people are often asking for the bare minimum changes so that they can continue their lives and access the education they are entitled to, and you can help with this.

Luckily, most changes that help Autistic people will also benefit everyone else, so you are unlikely to receive any pushback from the non-Autistic members of the student body. Quieter, less busy spaces are popular with all students wishing to work, and clearer instructions with specified deadlines help everybody. Making your university Autistic-friendly will allow your students to thrive in their academic environment. Training staff is paramount to collective understanding – this should not just be for the lecturers of specific Autistic students, but for everyone who works at the university. Autistic-led training is particularly useful, as Autistic people are experts in their own experience, and therefore will provide the greatest insight into what it is like to be an Autistic person at university.

Common adjustments that help Autistic people in lectures

- Being able to sit at the end of a row or at the back of the room.
- Reducing background noise.
- Clear lecture notes and comprehensive instructions for assignments and tasks.
- Access to an Autism expert or specialist study skills tutor.
- A quiet room where Autistic students can destress.
- Extended deadlines and longer to complete tasks in seminars.
- Not cold calling on students to answer questions in lectures.
- Teach all staff about Autism through Autistic-led training.

For Autistic people moving into the university, this can be an incredibly stressful time. To ensure they are happy and supported, consider what adjustments you need to make for them. Allowing Autistic students to arrive a few days early is incredibly important, and many universities are already offering this. Some universities allow Autistic students to move into their accommodation on the same day that the international students arrive. This does not add any additional pressure onto the university but will allow Autistic students to settle in and get to grips with their new surroundings before the obligations of the new term are upon them, and the rest of their flat moves in. Reach out over the summer to students who have disclosed that they are Autistic and offer them this adjustment. Some universities also hold meet-and-greets for Autistic students where they can meet members of the university support team or Autistic members of staff, as well as other Autistic students. This is very important, as research shows that having Autistic social connections can help Autistic people to feel connected, valued and included in their educational environments.

If you are in charge of flat allocation, think carefully about where your Autistic students will live. Having a flat that is near to university buildings and support services can help them to feel less alone, and mean they are more likely to reach out for support if they need it. Some students come to university looking forward to the social opportunities and will hold parties, stay up late, and play loud music. While some Autistic people may enjoy this, many would feel uncomfortable in this environment, so quieter halls may be best for them. Reach out and ask your students questions about whether they would prefer to live in dedicated quiet halls. Some universities also have no-alcohol halls, which can be perfect for people who do not drink for religious or other reasons.

Common adjustments for Autistic people living at university

- Arriving earlier at the start of the year.

- Being placed with students who requested a quiet flat.

- Not placing Autistic students in shared rooms or rooms where they need to move each term.

- Housing Autistic students together. This is not segregation – Autistic-only flats are not the goal here. However, research shows that Autistic people often enjoy the company of other Autistic people, so consider placing two Autistic students into the same flat.

- Having a dedicated quiet space.

- Being clear about when regular fire alarm testing will occur.

Autistic people generally have poorer health and mental health than non-Autistic people, and Autistic students will therefore likely need ongoing support while at university, and will need more support than their non-Autistic peers. Providing additional resources for Autistic students will benefit them, and, from a pragmatic view, will save resources in the future if you can prevent suspensions of study, dropouts and exam failure. Most universities offer a certain number of counselling sessions per student each year; consider offering Autistic students additional sessions, preferably with an Autism-trained counsellor. This should not be hard to fund as many students never take up their offers of counselling.

As mentioned previously, some universities have specific pages on their websites for Autistic students. These might have information about what support is available to them, common issues Autistic people might face such as **burnout** and social anxiety, and details of Autistic groups and peer support across the university. Again, learning from best practice is important, and if your university does not have such a webpage, look at what others are offering (examples on p.160) and ask Autistic staff and students what they need.

> **Common pastoral adjustments for Autistic students:**
> - Extra counselling sessions.
> - An Autism specialist counsellor.
> - Autism peer-support groups.
> - Clear signposting of Autistic support services and a dedicated webpage for Autistic students.

Autistic people may not need all, or any, of these adjustments, however it is useful is to provide them with a list of potential adjustments that they can pick from, and ask if there are any they wish to add. This is better than just asking 'What do you need?', as they may not think of the things they require on the spot, or not want to be an inconvenience or to be treated differently. Learning from best practice can help you to make your university a safer space for your Autistic students: ask colleagues throughout the university what they are doing to support their students, and investigate what other universities might be putting in place as well. Together we can make our learning spaces inclusive and comfortable for all students.

Peer support at university

Peer support for Autistic people was historically characterised by an older/more experienced non-Autistic person paired with an Autistic person; however, more people are realising that peer support can work better when both people have similar interests, experiences, and also neurotypes. The essentials of *peer* support must remain that it is peer support. Power imbalances must be avoided, and Autistic students must be acknowledged as experts in their own experience.

Setting up a group for neurodivergent people at your university can have great benefits for your staff and students. Research has shown the advantages of creating neurodivergent social groups, and spaces for neurodivergent people to interact. Your university may already have a staff neurodiversity network or similar, and many students' unions have disabled students' networks or even Autistic support networks. Consider how these different organisations could work together to bridge the gap between staff and students, and to share knowledge between learners. When setting up a group, consult with your Autistic colleagues and students to see what they would like to achieve, and what resources they require. Having a dedicated space for people to meet may not be possible, however having a *consistent* space will be better than one that changes on a regular basis, to allow for continuity and reduce stress for all those involved. Ensure that this space is safe, free from excessive noise, and close to facilities such as toilets and exits, comfy additions such as beanbags are a bonus but not essential. These groups should be relatively inexpensive to run; consider putting out refreshments such as tea, coffee and biscuits, to encourage people to attend. Fidget toys and board games may also be popular, but again, consult with neurodivergent people to see what sort of space and resources they need.

Consider who will run this group: if it is a group for students, it should be run by students, but university staff can assist in facilitating recruitment and advertising the group across the university. Finally, if it is an Autistic-specific peer-support group, consider who will be invited to attend and where students can find out about the group.

'Peer support is vital at university. However, developing and maintaining social relationships can be difficult for many Autistic people, particularly when in unfamiliar, busy environments. Due to the nature of the course I studied, I found friends who truly understand and accept me for who I am. Educators can help facilitate peer support by setting up buddy systems and offering online meet-ups before students join lectures. This can give students a chance to get to know each other in a safe space. Consideration should be given when planning pair and group work; roles should be clearly assigned, and the groups should be with people the Autistic person feels safe with.

Neurodiverse spaces could also be set up in the form of societies or virtual spaces. Being surrounded by people who experience similar challenges can help us feel less alone and misunderstood. A buddy could attend initial meetings to help widen social circles. It is important to recognise that for some Autistic people, socialising and masking to fit in can be exhausting and can lead to burnout. Therefore, it is vital that students are encouraged to socialise in their own way, at their own pace and quiet spaces are provided for downtime.

Lauren Smith, *Autistic student in Autism studies*

Tips for setting up Autistic peer support at your university:

- Consult with Autistic students and staff.

- Have a consistent space for groups to meet.

- Provide adequate resources and funding for the group to function.

- Consider recruitment and where the group will be advertised.

- Look at who will run the group, and avoid power dynamics by maintaining student involvement and leadership.

For further information on developing peer support, see work by the NEST Project at Edinburgh University (see details on p.190). This advice is primarily for schools, so would need to be adapted for the university setting.

What more can be done?

Overall, whatever your role at the university, you are reading this book because you want to help Autistic students get the most out of their time and prevent dropouts where possible. Taking the practical steps outlined in this chapter will help with this, but ultimately, many things will need to be implemented at a university-wide level. Therefore, if you can influence widespread change, increase awareness for those who think differently, and ensure accessibility and diversity are considered in all decisions and new schemes, this will help all students, neurodivergent or not, in having a better education. Look at university policies, and well-being campaigns, and scrutinise every paragraph, asking: is this in the best interests of our students?

Checklists and resources

Choosing a university

My essentials for a university:

-
-
-
-
-
-
-
-

My desirables for a university:

-
-
-
-
-
-
-
-

Universities to visit and open-day notes

University name	Date of open day	Notes from open day

What to pack

General	
☐ Laptop.	☐ Hangers.
☐ Clothes.	☐ A bag for lectures and shopping.
☐ Winter coat.	☐ A small bag for nights out.
☐ Winter boots.	☐ Laundry basket.
☐ Duvet and pillows.	☐ Mattress protector.
☐ Two sets of sheets for bed.	☐ Books.
☐ Blanket.	☐ Cuddly toy/s.
☐ Two big towels and two little towels.	☐ Extra blanket.
☐ Bathmat (check bathroom arrangement).	☐ Slippers.
☐ Toilet roll.	☐ New stationery.
☐ Hand soap.	☐ Emergency snacks.
☐ Condoms and lube.	☐ A small bin (if needed).
☐ Laundry bags.	☐
☐	☐
☐	☐
☐	☐
☐	☐

Cooking essentials
(for self-catered accommodation)

☐ Saucepan.	☐ Tin opener.
☐ Frying pan.	☐ Mug.
☐ Baking tray.	☐ Glass cup.
☐ Two chopping boards.	☐ Tea towels.
☐ Sharp knife.	☐ Washing-up gloves (if needed).
☐ Large plate.	☐ Sponges.
☐ Small plate.	☐ Washing-up liquid.
☐ Large bowl/pasta bowl.	☐ Kitchen spray.
☐ Small bowl/cereal bowl.	☐ Baking paper.
☐ Knife, fork and spoon (at least two of each).	☐ Cling film.
☐ Wooden spoon.	☐ Kitchen foil.
☐ Spatula.	☐ Sandwich bags.
☐ Sieve.	☐ Tupperware.
☐	☐
☐	☐
☐	☐
☐	☐

Your first shop

☐	Toilet roll.	☐	Washing liquid/powder (unless the machines are self-dosing).
☐	Hand soap.	☐	Fabric conditioner (unless the machines are self-dosing).
☐	Shower gel and shampoo.	☐	Tissues.
☐	Air freshener.	☐	

If in self-catered halls

☐	Washing-up liquid.	☐	Dried pasta.
☐	Sponges.	☐	Rice.
☐	Milk.	☐	Cereal.
☐	Butter.	☐	Jars of sauce (curry, pasta, tomato etc.).
☐	Bread x2 (stick one loaf in the freezer straight away).	☐	Tins of soup.
☐	Frozen pizzas.	☐	Cereal bars.
☐	Potatoes.	☐	

Admin checklist

☐	Insurance for your stuff.	☐	Had vaccinations.
☐	Signed rental contract.	☐	Have up-to-date passport and driving licence.
☐	Registered with a GP.	☐	Signed up for your modules.
☐		☐	

Physical health checklist

Sit down somewhere comfy and read through this list, trying to get in touch with your body and what it is feeling. Ask yourself:

- Do I feel hot or cold?

- Is my heart beating fast or slow?

- Can I take a nice deep breath if I want to? Does my chest hurt when I do?

- How does my stomach feel? Am I bloated, uncomfortable, or is it making noises?

- Do I feel sick? Hungry? Full?

- Am I hydrated? (The best sign for this is to look at the colour of your urine, it should be clear or slightly yellow.)

- Am I tired? Did I sleep well last night?

- Can I bend my arms and legs like usual? Are they stiff, sore or weak?

- Have I injured myself recently? Is it healing?

- Is my skin itchy? Do I have any dryness or rashes? Do I have any new marks or unusual spots?

- Do my teeth feel clean? Do I have toothache, or any areas of sensitivity?

- (If applicable) Have I had my period this month? Was it heavier/longer/more painful than usual?

- Have I taken my medication/supplements?

Start at your head and work down to your toes, asking:

■ Does this part of me hurt?

■ How much does it hurt out of 10?

Once you've completed this checklist, think:

■ Do I need to keep an eye on anything?

■ Do I need to ask for help?

Signs of meningitis and sepsis

In an emergency, call 999. If you are unsure about any symptoms, and it is not an emergency, call 111 (England, Wales and Scotland) or your GP.

The classic symptom was always cited as being a rash that doesn't disappear when a glass is pressed against it. However, this can be harder to see on darker skin types, and even if there is not a rash, trust your instincts and get emergency help if someone is experiencing symptoms.

Symptoms listed on the NHS website are:

- High temperature.

- Cold hands and feet.

- Vomiting.

- Confusion.

- Breathing quickly.

- Muscle and joint pain.

- Pale, mottled or blotchy skin (this may be harder to see on brown or black skin).

- Spots or a rash (this may be harder to see on brown or black skin).

- Headache.

- Stiff neck.

- Dislike of bright lights.

- Being very sleepy or difficult to wake.

- Fits (seizures).

Mental health checklist

Every day ask yourself, have I:

- Had a shower?

- Left my room?

- Cooked a meal?

- Talked to someone?

- Read something?

- Listened to my body?

- Drunk some water?

- Put on clean clothes?

- Brushed my hair?

- Cleaned my teeth?

If you are worried about someone, ask yourself whether they have:

- Had any changes in their sleep and/or eating habits?

- Been caring for themselves and their appearance as they usually do?

- Avoided social interactions they previously enjoyed?

- Taken part in any risky behaviours?

- Been more angry or frustrated than usual?

- Been abusing alcohol or other substances?

Autistic burnout signs

Consider this list to see if you are feeling or exhibiting any of these symptoms. There is space at the bottom where you can add your own symptoms or triggers. Understanding your triggers and signs of burnout can help you to avoid it happening, or to manage better when it is. There is a checklist you can fill in with a plan of what you will do if you start to become burnt out. Consider who you will reach out to in these instances, whether it be at the university, back home, or a helpline such as the Samaritans.

- Struggling to get out of bed.

- Needing more help than usual with cooking, cleaning, or doing the laundry.

- Thinking negative thoughts about yourself.

- Reacting more strongly to unpleasant stimuli like loud noises or bright lights.

- Feeling like you've lost social skills.

- Speaking less than usually, or going non-verbal when you were previously verbal.

- Being irritable.

- Struggling to remember things.

- Extreme tiredness and heaviness in your limbs.

My own signs of burnout:

-
-
-
-
-

My triggers (e.g. no day off, bright lights, certain activities):

-
-
-
-
-

When I am burnout out, or heading towards burnout, I will (e.g. have a hot shower, sit in the dark, let me lecturers know, reach out to counselling support):

-
-
-
-
-

Consent checklist

If you are worried about yourself or a friend, and whether they are able to consent to something, ask yourself: is the person...

☐ Sober of alcohol and drugs?

☐ Knowledgeable about the consequences of their actions?

☐ Aware of everything the situation entails?

☐ Old enough to consent to this action?

☐ Able to say no at any point, and reverse their consent?

☐ Not being coerced or manipulated into saying yes?

If you cannot tick off all of these things, they are not able to consent. Consent must be **freely given, informed, and reversible**, and the person must have **capacity** to consent.

Assignment planner

Assignment, e.g. Medieval poetry essay	Date due in	When I want to hand it in by	Tick when handed in

Essay structure

Start with your key points, three are written here, but you might be making more or fewer points.

Write out what you want to say for each point, with the references to back everything up.

Start writing each point; start in the middle and work outwards, writing your introduction and conclusion last.

Highlight a reference in your notes once you've used it in your essay, make sure you include all references.

Make sure you don't include any references for the first time in your conclusion.

- **Introduction**
  - Introduce the background to your essay and the points you are going to make.
- **Point/argument 1**
  - References and quotes
- **Point/argument 2**
  - References and quotes
- **Point/argument 3**
  - References and quotes
- **Discussion**
  - Bring together your points and discuss them.
- **Conclusion**
  - Don't mention anything here for the first time, any references you use here must have already been used before.

Reasonable adjustments

General

- [ ] Teach all staff about Autism, through Autistic-led training.
- [ ] Have dedicated quiet spaces across the university.

Academic

- [ ] Access to an Autism expert or specialist study skills tutor.
- [ ] A quiet room where Autistic students can de-stress.
- [ ] Extended deadlines and longer to complete tasks in seminars.
- [ ] Not cold calling on students to answer questions in lectures.

In lectures and seminars

- [ ] Being able to sit at the end of a row, or at the back of the room.
- [ ] Reducing background noise.
- [ ] Clear lecture notes and comprehensive instructions for assignments and tasks.

Pastoral

- [ ] Arriving earlier at the start of the year.
- [ ] Being placed with students who requested a quiet flat.
- [ ] Not placing Autistic students in shared rooms, or rooms where they need to move each term.
- [ ] Housing an Autistic student with another Autistic student.
- [ ] Being clear about when regular fire alarm testing will occur.
- [ ] Extra counselling sessions.
- [ ] An Autism specialist counsellor.
- [ ] Autistic peer-support groups.
- [ ] Clear signposting of Autistic support services and a dedicated webpage for Autistic students.

Access to Work

Things I think would make it possible for me to go to work,
or things that will mean I can work to my best ability:

☐

☐

☐

☐

☐

☐

☐

Recipe for gooey mug brownies

You can adapt this quite a lot and can add toppings or fillings such as chocolate chips as you wish. Flavourings like cinnamon or vanilla can also enhance it if you have these. You can double or even triple the ingredients if you have a particularly large mug.

You will need:

- [ ] 1 mug

- [ ] 1 large spoon butter

- [ ] 1 large spoon sugar (brown if you have it)

- [ ] 1 large spoon milk

- [ ] 1 large spoon cocoa power or hot chocolate powder

- [ ] 1 large spoon plain flour

Method:

1. Add the butter to the mug.

2. Melt the butter by sticking it in the microwave for 10-20 seconds (you might need a little longer if you are using a block of butter).

3. Add the other ingredients and stir.

4. Microwave for around a minute/minute and a half until it is bubbling.

Online resources

UCAS: www.ucas.com

Autism

National Autistic Society: www.autism.org.uk

NAS 'Starting University in England': www.autism.org.uk/advice-and-guidance/topics/transitions/england/starting-college-or-university

Estrangement

Stand Alone Charity: www.standalone.org.uk

Finance

Citizens Advice: www.citizensadvice.org.uk

Funding Higher Education for Disabled Students: www.disabilityrightsuk.org/resources/funding-higher-education-disabled-students

Applying for DSA:

General: www.disabilityrightsuk.org/resources/applying-disabled-students%E2%80%99-allowances-dsas

England: www.gov.uk/disabled-students-allowance-dsa

Scotland: www.saas.gov.uk/guides/disabled-students-allowance

Northern Ireland: www.nidirect.gov.uk/articles/financial-help-students-disabilities

Wales: www.studentfinancewales.co.uk/undergraduate-finance/full-time/tuition-fee-and-living-cost-students/what-s-available/disabled-students-allowance/

Mental health

Samaritans: www.samaritans.org
Call **116 123** for free (24/7). You can also email them, write them a letter, or pop into a local branch. The Samaritans were set up as a suicide prevention charity, but you do not need to be suicidal to call.

Peer-support programmes

In schools:

www.salvesen-research.ed.ac.uk/research/nest-neurodivergent-peer-support-toolkit

Fotheringham, F, Cebula, K, Fletcher-Watson, S, Foley, S & Crompton, CJ (2023), 'Co-designing a neurodivergent student-led peer support programme for neurodivergent young people in mainstream high schools'.

Renting

Your rights as a tenant:

- www.gov.uk/private-renting
- www.gov.uk/government/news/how-to-rent-as-a-student
- www.citizensadvice.org.uk/housing/renting-a-home/renting-from-a-private-landlord
- www.citizensadvice.org.uk/housing/renting-a-home/student-housing
- www.citizensadvice.org.uk/housing/renting-a-home/student-housing/students-in-university-accommodation/student-housing-rights-and-responsibilities-in-halls
- www.citizensadvice.org.uk/housing/renting-privately/ending-your-tenancy/getting-your-tenancy-deposit-back

Sex and relationship

Brook: www.brook.org.uk
Brook provides advice, free contraception, counselling, STI and pregnancy testing, and abortion referrals. Brook covers England, but links to services in the rest of the UK can be found on their website.

Terrance Higgins Trust: www.tht.org.uk
The Terrance Higgins Trust offers STI testing and support for people living with HIV. They also provide education and training in sex and relationships and run the National HIV Prevention Programme.

HPV and Smear tests: www.jostrust.org.uk

C-Card: Scheme to provide free contraception to young people. This is different depending on where you live. Search 'C-Card' and the name of your town or city, to find out about services near you.

Sexual assault

Rape Crisis England and Wales: call **0808 500 2222** for free (24/7), or live chat on their website www.rapecrisis.org.uk

Rape Crisis Scotland: Call 08088 01 03 02 (5pm-midnight) or live chat on their website www.rapecrisisscotland.org.uk

Rape Crisis Northern Ireland: Call 0800 0246 991 (Mon-Thurs, 6pm-8pm) or you can email through their website www.rapecrisisni.org.uk

Find a sexual assault referral centre (SARC) near you:

England: www.nhs.uk/service-search/other-health-services/rape-and-sexual-assault-referral-centres

Wales: Call Live Fear Free on **0808 80 10 800** (24/7) to find out where your nearest centre is, or visit //111.wales.nhs.uk/localservices/ and select 'sexual and reproductive health'

Scotland: www.nhsinform.scot/turn-to-sarcs

Northern Ireland: www.therowan.net/

University mentoring

Autism Mentoring at University: www.autism.org.uk/advice-and-guidance/professional-practice/mentoring-university

University complaints and compensation

England and Wales: Office of the Independent Adjudicator: www.oiahe.org.uk/

Scotland: Scottish Public Services Ombudsman: www.spso.org.uk

Northern Ireland: Northern Ireland Public Services Ombudsman: www.nipso.org.uk

Work

National Autistic Society: www.autism.org.uk/advice-and-guidance/topics/employment/support-at-work/autistic-adults

Access to work England, Scotland, and Wales): www.gov.uk/access-to-work

Employment Support (Northern Ireland): www.nidirect.gov.uk/articles/employment-support-information

Example webpages from universities

Durham University: www.durham.ac.uk/colleges-and-student-experience/student-support-and-wellbeing/disability-support/what-support-we-offer/autism-support/

Glasgow Caledonian University: www.gcu.ac.uk/currentstudents/support/disabilityservice/autism

London School of Economics and Political Science: https://info.lse.ac.uk/current-students/student-wellbeing/disability-wellbeing/autistic-spectrum-conditions

University of Cambridge: www.disability.admin.cam.ac.uk/working-disabled-students/autism-spectrum-conditions

University of Chichester: www.chi.ac.uk/student-life/support-health-wellbeing/disability-dyslexia-and-medical-conditions/autism-and-aspergers/